W0010763

To learn more about implementing the tools, processes and wisdom shared in this book, please visit www.TheNumbersEdge.com

First Edition
The Playbook to Managing Your Business by The Numbers
by Wesley Lindquist

ISBNs: 978-1-7341957-0-5 (paperback), 978-1-7341957-1-2 (hardcover), 978-1-7341957-2-9 (epub)

INTRODUCTION

Who Is This Book For?

In today's world of jam-packed schedules, filled with text messages and emails and calendar appointments buzzing all day on your smartphone—and sometimes even your wristwatch!—I'm sensitive to how important the efficient use of time is for all of us. That's why I designed *The Playbook To Managing Your Business By The Numbers* as a type of playbook to dispense the kind of information you might learn if your best friend were a CFO who invited you to coffee every week so he or she could teach you how to set up the accounting and finance side of your business and then guide you through understanding and using the information.

I'll be the first to admit that what you're going to read here isn't entirely original. What is unique, though, is having all these nuggets of wisdom available in one collection that walks you first through the basics and fundamentals of running a business by numbers, and then takes you further down that path by showing you ways to use the data to build strategies and take actions that increase profit and ensure the viability of your business.

Think of me and this book as a conduit for all the information I've gleaned from the great mentors I've been blessed to be around in my career, plus all of my experiences in business for the past two decades (and counting).

Interested?

This book will be most helpful for:

- First- and second-time business owners

- CEOs, business managers, and executives who have responsibility for improving the financial health of their companies

- Freelancers and solopreneurs, including those who have side businesses or home-based businesses

- Business owners who are either "also the bookkeepers" or the direct managers of the bookkeepers or controllers at their companies

- Bookkeepers, accountants, and controllers who want to improve their depth of knowledge, refine their expertise, and increase their skills at "thinking like a CFO."

How To Determine If This Book Is For You

If you answer "yes" to any of the following questions, this book is for you:

- Are you the founder or operations manager of your company, but don't have prior experience as a controller or CFO?

- Is there opportunity to improve your understanding of your company's Income Statement, Balance Sheet, and overall financial health?

- Is the crystal ball for the next few months of financial performance at your company hazy and only in your mind, rather than written down or captured on a spreadsheet?

- Are you too busy running the business to spend as much time as you want understanding your company's finances?

- Have you recently started a new business?

- Does the attention required to handle the financial side of your business take focus away from the main reason you started the business in the first place?

- Do you anticipate a future need for outside financing, such as a loan, line of credit, or investor?

- Could you benefit from guidance on how to manage your bookkeeper or head of accounting to get the most value out of that person and the information he or she provides?

- Do you feel you're leaving profit on the table, but aren't sure how to fix it?

How To Use This Book

There are real life lessons to be learned from experienced, enthusiastic CFOs who have been working with businesses of all sizes for many years—and that's what you gain access to with *The Playbook To Managing Your Business By The Numbers*. In it, I share tools, techniques, and practices built from hundreds of points of failure, success, and lessons learned.

- **Part One** of *The Playbook To Managing Your Business By The Numbers* is most applicable to new businesses. In it we explore the entity types you might choose for your company, the setup of your bookkeeping and accounting software, how to establish some key standard operating procedures, how to stay organized, and how to get your bookkeeping into a rhythm so it runs as smoothly as possible. This is the foundation, and because we intend to build a solid building— namely, your business—on top of this foundation, we need to be clear about what makes a strong foundation, put that foundation in place, and then turn our attention to what comes next. The foundation is only part one.

- **Part Two** explains how to review and understand the numbers that result from having a smooth bookkeeping system in place. We learn about each of the key financial statements, how to read them, how to arrange the look of them on the page, and what questions to ask. Understanding financial statements is akin to knowing how to read the architectural plans for your building. When you know what you are looking at and why the architect—or in the case of financial statements, your bookkeeper or accountant— drew them up that way, you are better prepared to ask for and get the financial results you desire.

- In **Part Three**, we look at how to use historical financial statements and information to look ahead, how to make your cloudy crystal ball clearer, and ways to integrate regular reviews of your crystal ball into the rhythm of managing your business. The main purpose of understanding historical financial and statistical information is to provide insight as to where the business is going. Future expectations should be written down, planned out, and managed to. Part three explains how veteran business owners manage their companies by the future and the forecast, not by the past, and how you can increase your success by doing the same.

- **Part Four** provides guidance about how experienced business managers can use their financial information and forecasts to build strategies and take action to increase profit, reduce the risk of one unfortunate event crippling their business, and accomplish their business goals. After all, the information gleaned from the first three parts of this book is only useful when it gets turned into action.

The Playbook To Managing Your Business By The Numbers shortcuts the path to success for small business owners by clearly explaining what to do and what not to do to gain an edge over the 90 percent of other small business owners who don't have adequate financial systems in place or the wherewithal to understand the information churned out by them. These are the plays experienced CEOs and/or CFOs would call when taking charge of a new business. Think of it as your admission ticket to the game!

Experience Is The Best Teacher

Running a business is a lot like raising a child. Just as parenting styles change as children age, the tactics used to run a company that has two or three employees aren't likely to be as effective when the company grows to 10 or 15 employees—and they may be totally ineffective when the company exceeds 40 employees. Just like a parent, as a business owner you need to go beyond the basics of nurturing   and caring and consistency to be able to grow your business into something you're proud of. You need to be flexible and you need to be able to adapt because everything doesn't always go as planned. When you can do that, both as a parent and as a business owner, you stand a much better chance of achieving desired results.

In my experience, one of the common qualities of businesses that achieve a reasonable amount of success is they have an owner who undergoes continuous self-improvement, actively identifies weaknesses that he or she turns into strengths over time, is keenly aware that there is a lot he or she doesn't know, and seeks advice and opinions from others with experience (just as parents seek advice, wisdom, and tips from other parents).

Every profession or technical discipline has a series of written or unwritten fundamentals that veterans of that profession use to maximize success. Consider these examples:

- An experienced baseball player knows the subtle rules for when to run and when to stay on base, or when to throw the ball to second base rather than third after catching a pop fly.

- An experienced restaurant manager knows the subtle rules for when to send wait staff home as the dinner crowd thins or when to reorder inventory to balance stretching cash vs. making sure the restaurant doesn't run out of a particular food or drink item.

Most of us would not know these fundamentals if we were to be dropped suddenly into a baseball game or asked to manage a restaurant. Similarly, because many business founders are first-time business owners, they don't have the benefit of experience to guide their decisions, which leads to a higher risk of failure and a reduced level of success.

Most business owners I know will tell you their success depends much more on the lessons they've learned in business than it does on their MBA . . . and I'm a perfect example. I have found that the kind of knowhow that comes from experience is almost always a better foundation for decision making than intuition, logic, or the theory taught in school.

My Story

I'm the kind of person who can go out with friends or colleagues and talk about business all night long and come away energized, sometimes to the frustration of others who were looking forward to leaving work at the office and putting as much mental distance as possible between their day and their night.

I've been a natural student of business for a long time. I grew up with parents and family members who started or ran numerous business with varying levels of success. I'm intrigued by how businesses operate. I'm captivated by their similarities and differences. I'm in awe of how challenging it is for some businesses to stay alive, while for others who get their recipe for success right, how common it is for the incomes of their owners to far surpass what their W2 incomes would have been if they worked for someone else.

I've been incredibly fortunate to have been surrounded by great mentors at the companies that hired me, and to have seen first-hand a variety of approaches and principles for running businesses successfully.

After graduating from college with an accounting degree, I started my career working for a well-run, $6 billion company that had a great accounting and finance department. I started as a temp with the company, then was hired as a full-time accounting assistant, got promoted to a staff accountant in the corporate office, and then was promoted to a financial analyst at one of the subsidiaries. I spent four great years with the organization under great mentors who regularly allowed me to be the youngest person in the room with senior management, offering the finance perspective when called upon. I worked under a CPA and studied during nights and weekends for two long years to earn my CPA.

My second, major post-college job was with a $400 million business consisting of a variety of companies and subsidiaries. There, too, I worked with great mentors, albeit in a business environment that was slow to change. I found myself leading and implementing most of what I had learned at my first employer, trying to change the culture from that of a 60-year old business to one that was more modern, agile, and efficient.

Teaching a company how to be better run while being supported by great executives gained me even more valuable experience as I learned from my own successes and mistakes rather than simply absorbing theory. While there, I went back to night school and earned my MBA, embracing business concepts and case studies like a sponge and bringing this knowledge back to the office where we'd consider integrating it into our operations.

Four years later, the next major chapter of my career took me to a $100 million construction and service company. There, I reported to a brilliant CFO who dedicated a seemingly unlimited amount of time to teach me everything he knew. I also spent a lot of time interfacing with partners at the private equity firm that owned us.

In just two years at this company, I gained more knowledge and experience than I had in my entire career to that point. The CFO set the tone with his bold, brazen, and effective candor. One of his favorite expressions, was "If we don't like the way we're doing something, let's change it and start tomorrow morning," which we often did. He opened my eyes to working in a business environment where we didn't have to keep doing things a certain way just because we always had.

Decisions became action quickly at this company. Any change we thought was the right decision to implement would be well on the way to achievement a week later. We closed the accounting books for 13 offices around the country by noon on day three every month. We managed our key performance indicators and the profitability on every project to the penny as part of the rhythm of the business. We were agile, efficient, logical, and made fast-paced decisions based on timely, accurate information.

On any given day, we were involved in over 100 construction projects around the country, with contract values between $250,000 -$5 million, plus dozens of smaller jobs. I knew what the expected profitability was on each project every day, and how each project's margins had changed from the week prior and from the original numbers that came out of our estimating department. Those leading every project knew which phases of every job were performing better than plan and which ones were not, and by exactly how much. We knew our finances and key performance indicators and managed our business by numbers as well as I'd ever seen anyone do it prior (and perhaps since). This business set the finance standard by which I would measure all companies I would work with in the future.

Unfortunately, in business, when your company can't generate the revenue and margin it needs to compete, knowing your numbers only allows you to get as far ahead of the decline as possible. I found out the hard way, as many did in 2009, that even when you know the numbers you can't always save the company.

We were in the construction business at a time of crushing recession for the construction and banking industries, and the country's economy overall. While we were able to maintain a million-dollar plus operating profit through the downturn, our Balance Sheet was saddled with a $40 million bank loan to buy out the previous owners, resulting in a principal and interest bill of $6 million a year. As the person in charge of forecasting, I knew we were in trouble when   my forecast showed we'd blow through our line of credit in just 15 months. Ouch.

To try to stay alive, we cut our overhead in half in less than a year. I had never experienced anything so swift and decisive in business. Cuts that deep and fast were major decisions our executive team handled assertively. Witnessing the tactics they used added to the growing treasure trove of experiential tools in my toolkit—tools that I could never have added without living through something firsthand. Even though the company had to close its doors eventually, I consider that experience to be my second MBA.

This led to the fourth major chapter of my professional career, which by itself brought a wealth of business experience that went exponentially beyond all of my prior experiences combined.

Fatigued by working for companies that ran their businesses through spreadsheets, theory, and long-term strategies, I was thirsty for something a bit more tangible. I decided to connect with a young, passionate, up-and-coming consulting firm full of A-Players that was eager to bring big business accounting and financial management practices to small companies.

Shifting my focus to work with small businesses was exactly the change I needed—a change that aligned perfectly with my passion for finding little ways to make big differences in a company's or business owner's finances. (For example, when working with a small business, even finding a way to increase the bottom line by $10,000 can allow a business owner to take his or her family on a vacation they couldn't otherwise afford.)

As part of this consulting firm, I worked as the part-time consultant CFO or controller for dozens of businesses, big and small, across a wide range of industries for six years, transforming them from companies whose bookkeeping was in shambles (or non-existent) to companies that were receiving financial wisdom and analysis more insightful than most $100 million companies with big finance departments were getting.

For my first two years there, our team worked to craft our definition of quality accounting and financial management, teaching our staff to operate under world class standards and practices. Within six years, this approach grew our own headcount and revenue more than 500 percent!

In my time at this consulting firm, I saw the lives of dozens of business owners change for the better, with many of my clients selling their companies for well over $100 million in the aggregate. I came to thoroughly understand how banking and lending works, completing 10 to 15 loan transactions a year. I played an integral part in growing businesses exponentially over a period of years. By implementing cash flow management practices and helping owners understand and make expense reduction decisions, I was able to save a number of businesses from closing their doors.

Best of all, I got to learn from great mentors and gain more experience than most CFOs would hope to gain in a lifetime. I consider this experience to be my third MBA.

Ultimately, I have always known the best role for me is to be a business owner, which is an unusual place for a trained accountant. Leadership and business strategy have always been more fun to me than the actual nuts and bolts of accounting, though I will always value being an expert in the common language of all businesses.

Over the years, I've started three businesses with missions, visions, and cultures consistent with my style, experience, and personality. All were based on a genuine desire to help as many business owners around the world "win" using my experiences and whatever wisdom I have acquired during my career.

I like helping other people win, and I like to see the results. That's what motivates me. As a life-long student of business, I acknowledge the irony of feeling gratified when I help others win, but at some point in my career, I recognized that by helping *others* succeed, I didn't have to worry about my own success because it would naturally follow. The result is getting to live a life and pursue a career doing exactly what I love. To me, that's success.

I know running a business is challenging, frustrating, and stressful. Lots and lots of business owners have less success than their potential—probably the majority. And even when a business does well, it's rarely comfortable for more than a year or two until the goalpost moves or when fear sets in because you're worried your competitors will have an advantage on you.

I also know that most businesses come up short or fail after start up due to the inability of their owners to identify and focus on fundamentals that will ensure their businesses stick around for the long-term. It's precisely these prerequisites and processes necessary to manage a business by numbers that *The Playbook To Managing Your Business By The Numbers* covers . . . and once managing your business this way becomes part of the rhythm of your company, you'll never want to run another business again without this playbook and its teachings in place.

Leveling Up

Before we dive right into our first foundational discussions about the business and financial management needs of companies, I want to introduce the concept of "Levels" when referring to the maturity of a business. Levels are a subjective description of the relative size and complexity of businesses, beginning with the smallest and newest of entities (Level 1, including businesses where the owner is the only employee) up through companies that own multiple subsidiaries or sister companies and may have hundreds of employees (Level 4).

Understanding how levels of businesses are referenced will facilitate an understanding of which strategies are appropriate for which situations because many strategies that are appropriate for Level 1 and Level 2 businesses are not as applicable to Level 3 and Level 4 companies, and vice versa.

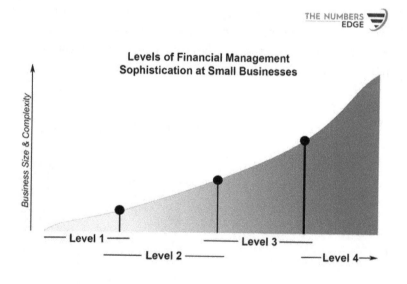

Level 1 Businesses

Most businesses start out small, perhaps with only one employee. When a business is small, the finances are tangible. The money is easily controlled by the CEO, who sees every cash transaction going in and out. I call these Level 1 businesses.

Much of the information presented in this book is highly applicable to Level 1 businesses. We also have lots of training videos, written guidance, checklists, and templates available for Level 1 business owners on our website at www.TheNumbersEdge.com.

Level 1 businesses:

- Need to have someone doing the bookkeeping who understands the minimum fundamentals necessary to maintain appropriate records

- Might have the owner doing the bookkeeping or it might be outsourced, depending on the aptitude and interest of the owner

- Are at high risk to run out of cash and go out of business

- May not have established a proven recipe for success

- Have not implemented ways to scale the business.

Critical financial management functions include the following:

- Knowing the current and future cash position

- Understanding the basics each month about whether the health of the business is improving or deteriorating.

We offer a CFO Membership program that's popular with Level 1 business owners. This includes full access to all of our tools and templates at www.TheNumbersEdge.com, a dedicated line for asking an expert CFO about bookkeeping and finances, and a monthly phone or video meeting with your dedicated CFO at The Numbers Edge. Our CFO Membership program is like having a CFO for a best friend—someone who keeps you on the right path and is available for questions and guidance.

A common transition point for when a business outgrows Level 1 is around five to 10 employees.

Level 2 Businesses

Businesses that add employees, revenue, and complexity during the Level 1 stage graduate to delegate the bookkeeping to another person (hopefully, someone who is a trained bookkeeper). At this stage, the business owner needs to manage a bookkeeper rather than manage the bookkeeping. Bookkeeping for a Level 2 business is a part-time job.

Level 2 business owners:

- Have a part-time bookkeeper

- Need to be receiving regular information from the bookkeeper to maintain the best understanding of the company's financial health, such as weekly Accounts Receivable and Accounts Payable reports, monthly financials, and possibly a weekly short-term cash flow forecast.

In Level 2 businesses, without regular monitoring, cash can trickle out unnoticed. This can increase the likelihood that the CEO

gets an unwelcome surprise when he or she learns the business's financial health has deteriorated.

As businesses graduate from Level 1 to Level 2, selecting the right bookkeeper is a critical decision. The Numbers Edge website is full of guidance about how to interview and hire bookkeepers, what type of bookkeepers are available in the marketplace, and more. We know virtual bookkeepers who work for businesses all around the country and are always happy to make introductions.

A common transition point for a business to outgrow Level 2 is around 15 to 30 employees.

Level 3 Businesses

When you're in charge of a Level 1 and sometimes a Level 2 business, you get to see practically all of the cash flow in and out of the business because you're personally signing checks or releasing electronic payments. With a Level 3 business, owners must begin to manage their businesses by numbers, reports, and metrics. Maintaining a hands-on understanding of the finances of the business simply by being the one who signs the checks no longer works at this stage.

A Level 3 business:

- Has a full-time bookkeeper at the company, and possibly additional accounting staff

- Has a part-time controller or part-time CFO who determines the best data and numbers to be watching as leading financial health indicators

- Has a controller or CFO who is guiding the CEO and others

17

on how to interpret the numbers on a weekly or monthly basis, and should be meeting with the CEO regularly to ensure everyone is aligned with how the financial health of the company is trending

- Should maintain their finances as though a bank or investor were providing capital to the company

- Should close its books promptly each month with insightful financials provided to the business owner

- Should run its accounting according to checklists and standard operating procedures

- Should emphasize the Balance Sheet as an important business tool

- Should strategize regularly about how to improve gross margin, minimize overhead, and maximize profit

- Should have a line of credit with a bank to decrease risk and provide capital in the event of an unexpected positive revenue opportunity or negative setback.

For Level 3 businesses with a solid accounting team, the CFO Membership program through The Numbers Edge website is an inexpensive, helpful way to fine-tune best practices and provide light guidance and oversight to your controller.

For those companies requiring a more hands-on approach (which is most common for Level 3 businesses), we also offer an excellent virtual CFO program where an experienced CFO looks over your books monthly in depth, meets with your head of accounting to provide guidance on recommended improvements to your

accounting program and financial reporting, and meets monthly with the CEO or management team by phone or video conference to present the highlights of the financial health of your business.

A common transition point for a business to outgrow Level 3 is around 50 to 100 employees.

Level 4 Businesses

A Level 4 business needs a full-time, capable and experienced controller, or in some situations at least a part-time CFO. Level 4 companies have multiple people on their accounting staff and need to be mindful of accounting team career paths and employee retention.

At a Level 4 company:

- The accounting work is more time-consuming and complex and could involve multiple revenue streams or multiple business entities.

- Monthly financial reports may be 10 or more pages, should include a Statement of Cash Flows, should be insightful enough to impress sophisticated investors or bankers, and should clearly reflect the story of the operations of the company.

- The business is large enough so that having experienced financial leadership could be the difference in earning or losing tens of thousands (or even hundreds of thousands) of dollars.

- The CEO needs to be thoroughly familiar with how to read financial statements.

- Understanding the Balance Sheet is critically important, as the Balance Sheet is the supreme measure of the financial health of the business.

- Management should use forecasts and budgets and should be looking ahead constantly, "driving by seeing out the windshield rather than through the rearview mirror."

We support Level 4 businesses through our Virtual CFO service, which you can learn more about at www.TheNumbersEdge.com. If your company doesn't have the level of talent it needs on its accounting team, we often participate in the interview and recruiting process to help you get the right team members in place. Our experienced CFOs are thoroughly familiar with Level 4 companies, including those who need immediate or turnaround help in their cash or financial situations.

PART ONE

"You can't build a great building on a weak foundation. You must have a solid foundation if you're going to have a strong superstructure."
- Gordon B. Hinckley

THE FUNDAMENTALS FOR
NEW BUSINESSES

The fundamentals of business financial management covered in this book are especially applicable for businesses that are just opening their doors. These fundamentals also can act as a checkup for any small business that wants to make sure there are no missing keystones in its financial management foundation.

If everything we're going to talk about here is working well at your company, that's great. This is the easy stuff that every business should be doing. If your company is missing on a few of these, don't fret. A majority of small business owners, like you, started their businesses based on a particular skill, talent, or passion rather than any kind of business expertise.

In fact, nearly all successful business owners admit they only developed greater business management acumen *after* startup, once they realized there was a void in their expertise. Once this gap was identified, the business owners who then decided to learn the fundamentals and understand their numbers early in the life cycles of their businesses became better able to reduce mistakes, risk, and anxiety compared to others.

In my experience as a CFO for dozens of companies, I have come to believe firmly and unequivocally that business owners who understand their finances have a competitive advantage over those who do not. They have a greater likelihood of financial success and are at a reduced risk of going out of business due to running out of cash unexpectedly. I consider this fundamental level to be the minimum acceptable standard of business financial management knowledge and understanding required for anyone to run a company effectively.

Can business owners who don't know anything about finance achieve great success?

Absolutely. There are lots of important factors for achieving great success. Having a great business model combined with a profitable and effective sales and marketing funnel leads many businesses to enviable levels of success, at least to a certain point of growth and size.

Can great business owners who know their numbers go out of business?

Absolutely. Unfortunately, it happens surprisingly often for many reasons.

However, nearly any business in any industry can achieve at least some level of success by following the fundamentals of good business management. That said, let's start with the fundamentals for founders of brand-new businesses.

Building Your Roadmap

You will soon discover that most of the discussion in this book revolves around guidance you would expect to get from a CFO, filled with common threads about increasing profits, understanding finances, and managing by numbers. But before we get into all of that, we first need to look at the most important consideration of all for any business owner: YOU.

- What are your goals for the business and for yourself personally?

- Why do you have this business, and how do you hope it will help you reach those goals?

- What do you want this business to be like in a year, two years, five years, or beyond?

- What do you want your lifestyle, your income, and your accomplishments to be at each of these milestones?

Businesses get started for lots of different reasons. Different business owners set out to take different paths, use different roadmaps, and end up at different destinations.

If you haven't thought through your "roadmap," take out a piece of paper and write down what comes to mind. Having some kind of plan, goals, or direction is critical for helping you achieve a desired level of success, especially when you can define what it looks like to reach your objectives or milestones.

With each business I started, only after some time was I really able to articulate clearly what my goals had been all along. I found that my goals changed along the way, either due to personal circumstances or because I achieved a certain amount of success and decided to move my goalposts.

In starting a business, this important first step isn't about defining a goal, writing it in stone, and sticking to it forever. What's important is that you have a conversation with yourself early on so you have an idea of where you want to go, what you want the business to become, and what you want to avoid.

For most small business owners, success isn't measured by the net income the company earns. It's defined by the extent to which the business owner is accomplishing his or her goals. Your goals are your plan. If you're already running your business without a plan, now is the time to give some consideration to why you are here and where you want to be.

Many years ago, I worked with a business whose tagline was "Plan, execute, achieve," which is an excellent parallel to this book's overarching theme of maximizing success. In my experience, the most successful business owners tend to be those who start with a plan, which they execute in a way they believe will accomplish that plan, which then leads to them being able to achieve their desired results.

Easy, right?

I work with a CEO who describes his goals and planning as follows: "I know where I am now, and I know where I want to get to in the future. I don't naturally get caught up in the in-between. I'm always focused on the solutions needed to reach the end goal. I think in terms of two timeframes: now (on the left) and the end (on the right)."

Now   The Goal

My approach works a little differently. I'm more of a "one step at a time" person. While I certainly could articulate the ultimate goal I'd like to achieve if someone pushed me for an answer, I'm naturally much more tactical. I inherently focus on the tactics of the first major milestone, with an almost paranoia-like worry that I won't be able to get there.

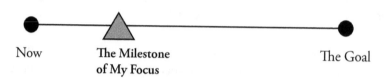

| Now | The Milestone of My Focus | The Goal |

Neither approach is right or wrong—and if you don't have a big, lofty, ultimate goal that may or may not be achieved, that's fine.

In the initial planning, you might write down goals like these:

- I'd like to replace my salary in my previous job, plus 20 percent, within four months.

- I'd like to spend more time with my kids without having to compromise my current lifestyle.

- I'd like to retire by a certain age and I'm willing to work hard until then to get there.

- I'd like to know that my financial future is taken care of.

- I'd like to work with my friends, have fun, earn a good living, and not overburden myself with stress.

For my business, The Numbers Edge, which includes this book and the website, www.TheNumbersEdge.com, one of my goals is "to help as many business owners as possible maximize their success by avoiding preventable mistakes and implementing processes that enhance success, through a format that is easy to share with the world."

A secondary goal of mine is "to be able to point those who ask me for advice on these topics (which happens ALL the time!) to information I've already put into a format they can easily access, which allows me to have more time available for family."

Notice that my goals around my business are not related to a particular size or profit, which is ironic, I suppose, since I am by profession a numbers guy. For me, my goals are more about reaching certain targets that, if I attain them, will provide me with levels of pride and satisfaction that others might achieve only by attaining financial goals.

Again, there is no right or wrong approach. I provide these examples as illustrations to take any complexity or fear out of the process of looking inward and asking yourself what you are doing here, what you expect in return from all of the hours you will spend in the coming years working in your business, and whether there is an outcome in the future you hope to attain. Just know that not all goals need to be financial in nature, though many are.

So, in the first steps of applying what all great business leaders consider fundamental, take a few minutes and jot down some ideas about your purpose and your hope for the future. Brainstorm. Don't worry about what format your idea is in. Just write whatever comes to mind.

As you do, you may discover some words that explain why your business exists and what you want the future for it to be. If you can fit those words into a sentence or two, and perhaps clean it up to sound just a touch more formal, this might turn out to be what is traditionally referred to as the mission (purpose) and vision (future) of your business.

- If the mission of your business is to create a nice income for yourself and your business partner while having some fun along the way, that's great. You probably wouldn't publish that to your team or customers before making it sound a little more selfless, but at least you've defined the purpose of working in the business every day.

- If your plan is to create a company that can be sold to another party for a lot of money, you can now be more mindful of whether your ongoing business decisions support that objective or hinder it.

Before moving on to some more tactical topics, I'll leave you with some wisdom from one of my many mentors, who is fond of saying, "What do you call a plan that is not in writing? *Not a plan.*"

Entity Type

If you haven't already set up a separate legal entity for your business, and if you intend to, you should do it early. This saves administrative time later on from having to file or modify paperwork or contracts, and you'll receive the benefits of having that legal entity structure set up sooner.

Many new business owners complete this step before their first customer, first transaction, or first bank account—which is ideal if you can arrange it in that order, but it doesn't always happen that way. Many businesses start out as freelancers providing services or developing simple products to sell, and then create separate entities only after they've gained some traction and optimism that their initial steps are developing into sustainable businesses.

If you're generating revenue and you haven't set up a separate legal entity for your business, you are by definition either a sole proprietor (if you're the only one in business) or a partnership (if there are multiple founders of the company all working together). That's the default if you don't have any paperwork indicating otherwise. As a sole proprietorship, the owner and the business are one intertwined unit from the perspective of the law and the tax rules.

When you create a **separate entity** and all of your business transactions flow in and out of that other entity, the owner and the business become two legal entities. That creates some benefits, and some areas that require careful consideration, compared to operating as one unit.

Some points you'll want to consider when determining the optimal business entity for you include the following:

- What type of situations could create a risk of the business being sued? Could someone trip and fall and get injured on your property? Could someone accuse you of causing damage to their own family or business? If so, by having your business as a separate legal entity, the only assets someone suing could potentially take in a worst case scenario are the assets of the business—not your personal assets (since you and the business are separate). Separating legal liability between the business and the owner is one of the main reasons entrepreneurs use separate legal entities rather than sole proprietorships for their businesses. (It's important to understand that simply creating a separate entity does not by itself insulate the owner from all liabilities of the business, and that certain activities and behaviors could result in a court "piercing the corporate veil"—meaning to disallow the intended separation between business and personal. This usually happens only when the business entity and the owner's personal situation are more commingled than separated.)

- If the business and the owner are now two separate legal entities, how can money move between them without creating a taxable transaction? In some forms of business entities, passing money from the business to the owner can result in taxes being owed. In other entity types, funds can flow freely between the owner and the business.

Based on the expected level of profitability, the overall taxes due on income will be different based on the entity type selected. If three businesses all earn $100,000 in taxable income this year, the taxes due will be different if the company is a **C-Corp** vs. a **sole proprietorship** vs. an S-Corp (where the business owner only reports half of the taxable income through payroll and receives a distribution of profits for the other half).

There are a couple of potential downsides about separating the business from yourself:

- First, as two separate entities, there may be two different tax returns that need to be prepared, which would result in additional tax preparation fees.

- Second, some states charge an annual fee to keep a separate legal entity open for your business.

Add these two considerations together and you may find that in some situations having a separate legal entity could cost you more than a $1,000/year in fees beyond what would be required if the business were a sole proprietorship. For some situations, that cost isn't worth the benefit.

What's The Right Entity For You?

There is a mass of literature available online about how to choose an entity type, and any reasonable CPA or attorney should be able to outline the pros and cons of each for your situation. This book isn't intended to direct you towards the entity structure that is ideal for your particular situation. My goal is simply to provide some context for why choosing the appropriate entity type is an important fundamental of starting a small business and perhaps raise a few questions for you to consider when doing your own research or working with a CPA or attorney.

I do, however, want to point out some general guidelines concerning entity types that are based on my experiences working with small businesses over the years:

1. For most small businesses that have one owner or a couple of owners, that have less than 50 employees, and

that generate less than $500,000 in net income annually, it is not common for them to choose a C-Corp as the optimal entity structure. When a C-Corp passes money to its owner(s), those transactions are usually taxable. At most small businesses, one of the main objectives is to get money to the owners, and more wealth can be built if that transaction happens in a tax-free way.

2. Owners of many Level 1 to Level 3 businesses (see definitions of business levels in the "Leveling Up" section of the introduction) might want to ask their tax experts whether the ideal structure would be first to create an LLC and then file paperwork with the IRS to be taxed as if the business were an S-Corp. This offers some benefits of having an LLC rather than actually having an S-Corp (lower administrative requirements), and in some situations can result in lower payroll taxes, potentially saving up to a few thousand dollars a year.

3. A business can also have a name for marketing purposes that is different from the entity's legal name. For example, the entity might be called "Jennifer Fitness, LLC," but the name you want on the sign, and that you want your customers to know you by, might be "Get in Shape Fitness." To accomplish this, you fill out simple paperwork with your state to create a "doing business as" name (or DBA). You can have multiple DBAs for one company. Customers can make payments to the name of your DBA and your bank will accept those payments under the legal name of your company. DBAs are easy and inexpensive to get.

Choosing a business entity type is a good example of why it is important for business owners to identify experts they trust in a business advisory or consultation role, such as an attorney, tax preparer or accountant. Most business owners find that from time to time they need to bounce ideas or ask questions of someone who has relevant technical expertise.

At The Numbers Edge, that's part of why we created our CFO Membership program—to give business owners an easy, inexpensive way to establish a relationship with a CFO they trust to be a sounding board and to point out opportunities and risks that might otherwise be overlooked. Our CFO Membership program is like having "a best friend that's a CFO." To learn more, go to www.TheNumbersEdge. com.

Entity Governance

After you set up the entity, it is customary to set up some rules regarding the governance of the entity. In an LLC, this is done through the operating agreement. In a corporation, this is done through a shareholder agreement. While not all states require that these documents be filed, you should create them for your business anyway. Again, check with an expert.

Segregating Business from Personal

Any experienced small business accountant will tell you that when a business owner commingles business and personal transactions in the same bank account or credit card account, it's a terrible situation. It leads to reduced precision in company accounting, which drives accountants crazy and exposes the business owner to risk in the event of an IRS audit or some other kind of investigation by a financially literate third party.

One fundamental of running a business is to set up a separate bank account and credit card that you use exclusively for business transactions. It doesn't matter if the accounts actually happen to be in your personal name, especially for a business credit card, because you're not likely to get a credit card based solely on business credit early on. The important point is to use separate bank and credit card accounts for business transactions only, and to keep all your personal transactions out of these accounts.

This rule applies whether your business is a sole proprietorship or a separate legal entity. The important part isn't about whether all of your accounts are opened in the name of your business (though if you have a separate legal entity, your bank accounts should be in the business name and tax ID). This is about keeping your business transactions entirely separate from your personal transactions. Commingling transactions between business and personal items in the same account leads to bookkeeping nightmares quickly, and in the unlikely scenario of an IRS audit, demonstrates a lack of bookkeeping and financial discipline that can work against you.

In the infrequent occurrence where a transaction that is entirely personal, which should not appear on the business tax return as a business expense, does come through a company bank account or credit card, the bookkeeper should know to treat that transaction as a receivable that the owner needs to pay back or that, in some cases, can be classified as a distribution of profits to the owner. Note that with some entity types or business situations, a company cannot make distributions of profits to the owner or the distribution could be a taxable transaction.

Here's a great (and very simple) rule to follow: always pay for business expenses out of the business account and personal expenses out of a personal account. Make it standard procedure, a no-brainer. If the owner needs to transfer funds from the business to cover a personal cash need, that's strongly preferable to just paying for the personal cost directly from the business account—even if the transaction was to be recorded as a receivable that the owner needs to pay back.

In reality, personal charges do occasionally hit the business account. Sometimes the cardholder uses the wrong card. Sometimes the business owner initially thinks a transaction might be business-related but ultimately decides it's personal instead. Here are how transactions should be recorded in those situations:

- If a transaction is truly a business expense by definition of the IRS and expected to be tax deductible, it gets recorded to the expenses section of the business.

- If a transaction is personal, it is recorded as a receivable from the owner or, if you're sure that this is the appropriate treatment for your company, it could be recorded to distributions.

- Sometimes a transaction can be considered "in-between"— it's going to be tax deductible for the IRS, but it's really more personal than business in nature, so it wouldn't really be appropriate to see business operating expenses go higher in a given month just because of this. An example might be if the owner of the company has a meeting in Europe but gets in a day or two early and stays a day or two later, charging those costs to the company. Another example might be an owner who goes on a trip with a friend who also is a customer or potential customer (so it should be expensed, because they discussed business topics on the trip) but the primary reason of the trip really was pleasure. In these situations, the transaction should be coded as an "Other Expense," down below the Net Operating Income line of the income statement. This way the tax accountant will pick it up for the tax return, but the net operating income and the Selling, General & Administrative (SG&A) expense of the company won't be impacted by it.

Accounting Software

Every company needs to track its business income and expenses. There are lots of software products available for this purpose. Unless you have a reason to decide otherwise, when you start out you should use QuickBooks. QuickBooks has desktop (QuickBooks Desktop) and internet-based versions (QuickBooks Online). Either is initially fine.

QuickBooks Online can be navigated with minimal initiation and it has integrations to connect with lots of other software. QuickBooks Desktop (which can also be hosted in the cloud so you can access it from anywhere) is the choice of power users who value speed and efficiency when working in the software.

I'm not saying other software can't do the job by not mentioning other options here. If you know what you're doing and you have a reason to select something other than QuickBooks, then go for it. But if you don't have a reason to choose an alternative, QuickBooks has some advantages over the rest of the field:

- It's very widely known and used. Most outsourced bookkeepers, controllers, and tax preparers know it intimately. Hiring staff or consultants who are experienced with QuickBooks will be easy for you as the company grows.

- It's easy to troubleshoot most challenges with a Google search or a call to the QuickBooks support line.

- It does what it is supposed to do. It works when used correctly. You can't say that about all software.

- It's scalable. It works for very small businesses and can also run the accounting for some types of companies with $20 million (or more) in annual revenue.

If you're choosing QuickBooks Online, you need to select a version. To do the bookkeeping the right way at your company, you need a version that includes "manage bills." This allows vendor invoices to be tracked in the system, which will give you helpful information about what payments need to be made by what dates. (As of the time of this writing, this version is called the "Essentials" version of QuickBooks Online.)

When you're working with either version of QuickBooks (Desktop or Online), you can connect your bank accounts and credit card accounts directly to it so that transactions download automatically rather than needing to be keyed individually. Again, this underscores the need to use separate bank and credit card accounts for business transactions vs. personal transactions. By consistently separating business and personal transactions you'll know, for example, without having to think about it that Amazon purchases on the business card are always and only for business, and you won't need to divide and record transactions between business and personal expenses.

Staying Organized

Founders of businesses are usually juggling a wide variety of priorities—more than most regular employees. From sales prospects to compliance or tax deadlines, to marketing initiatives and meetings with others, staying organized is as important for small business owners as any other profession.

As a small business owner, you need a process to prevent the little things from falling through the cracks—a process that can grow with you as the company expands and the complexities increase.

Here are some of the tools the team at The Numbers Edge loves:

Receipt Tracking

Every credit card receipt should be saved as a habit and routine. In reality, if you don't save a receipt that's under $75, the IRS won't come after it. Nevertheless, it's easier to build a discipline of keeping all receipts than to be loose and inconsistent about the process.

Following the Six Sigma principles of consistency and simplicity, it is a lot simpler to have a single process that applies to all situations (for example, every time a credit card receipt is available it should be archived) than to have sub-rules for the situation with varying processes for each. For businesses that just have a single cardholder or a couple of cardholders, try this: set up a folder on Dropbox called "Receipts." Then, every time you get a credit card receipt use the Dropbox app on your phone to take a picture and save it to that folder. That way, you don't need to keep the hardcopy of the receipt.

If your transaction happens to be a restaurant bill, be sure to always document what makes the expense "ordinary and necessary" in the course of your business. I usually write things such as "Meeting with Nicole about ABC Company's March financial statements" or "Sales meeting with John, the CEO of Acme" at the top of the receipt before I capture it with my Dropbox app. This captures the reason for the expense with the source document. I always file my receipts with the file name "YYYY-DD-MM VendorName.pdf " so the files naturally appear in chronological order and are easy to find when needed.

Whether it's receipts or vendor bills or compliance paperwork or financial statements, I recommend you get in the habit early of filing everything electronically rather than keeping paper. Paper is such a hassle. It requires a space to hold it, a process for when to destroy it, and searching through it to find one piece of information is more time consuming compared to an electronic records search.

Our business keeps zero paper. If paper is the only way to get information, we run it through the scanner and destroy the hardcopy. When someone tries to give me a hardcopy document, my standard response is "I don't do well with paper." It's true! I don't have methods to file and organize paper, and it requires an extra step to scan it. I always ask if the person can send me an electronic version of the document instead of the paper version.

If your business is already so large that the Dropbox scan method won't work, take a look at Expensify or Concur, or ask others you trust for a referral to a more robust paperless system.

Event & Note Tracking

I take notes on everything, all the time, even though I have a good memory for a lot of details. I simply have way too much going on to keep it all in my head reliably. I'm just not 100 percent sure that, if needed, I could retrieve with total accuracy what was said or agreed to in a given situation. So, any time I enter a meeting, I immediately open my laptop to take thorough notes.

The people who have worked for me over the years who have struggled to be successful are often those people who don't naturally take good notes. Have you ever had a new employee come in for training, sit down, and not pull out a notebook or even a pen? I have. Be the opposite of that person. You want your experiences, meetings, and learnings all to become part of your toolkit, to make you better, and to give you history that you can reference along the path to continuous improvement.

I use Evernote for my note taking. My Evernote has thousands of notes. In fact, I wrote this book using Evernote. It synchronizes between all of my computers and devices, auto-saves what I'm writing constantly, has the functionality to selectively share my notes and notebooks so others can contribute, and allows me to organize and categorize my notes easily.

OneNote also works well and has similar functionality.

I tell people that I use Evernote for everything that has happened in the past, and I use Trello to plan things I need to do in the future.

Trello manages my punch lists for everything. It is highly collaborative, easy to use, has drag-and-drop functionality, and in the year since I've started using it, I have only needed the free version.

Imagine you have a huge, dry erase board. With a marker you draw vertical lines to separate the board into columns. To the head of each column you attach a label, such as "High Priority" or "Roadblocked" or "Already Completed." Beneath each label, you then use post-it notes to track the various things that need to be done. You might move a note from "Roadblocked" to "High Priority" once that bottleneck is cleared, and then to "Already Completed" when it's done. That's what Trello does, but virtually rather than with a dry erase board and post-it-notes. (I believe the Planner function in Microsoft Office 365 may be similar.)

Other Favorites

- I keep all of my passwords in LastPass, which also allows me to selectively share passwords with others. I can leave my LastPass open and hit the one-touch "Launch" button to open the website I'm going to, and it will log me in with just a single click. I can access and use my LastPass database from my smartphone and tablet. It works well for individuals and companies. I've also dabbled in Okta, which seems pretty similar to LastPass and has a good reputation.

- The majority of miles I put on my car are for business because I drive to meet with a lot of accountants and business owners as a consultant and part-time CFO. I'm well aware that the IRS requires mileage tracking when using a business vehicle for a mix of personal and business use, and I care about maximizing the tax deduction I can get when I use my car. I use an app on my phone that automatically recognizes when I start driving and tracks the miles traveled by segment. It then allows me to categorize each trip as business or personal, which I do by reviewing the history of my trips every couple of days. The app is called Everlance. Even though I hate paying for apps and software when the free version will do, I use the paid version of Everlance. It's well worth it for my situation. If you use a vehicle for both business and personal use, you need some kind of process for recording how many miles were for business travel that will be reasonably supportive if you're ever challenged by the IRS. Like accounting, filing, and other administrative tasks, it needs to take minimal effort rather than be a burden on your schedule or a frustration to use. For me, Everlance fits this requirement.

OTHER STARTUP FUNDAMENTALS

When starting a company, there are numerous decisions a business owner needs to make and steps to take to establish standards, processes, and routines. We covered some of the basics in the previous chapter. In this chapter, let's take a look at a few more.

How Will You Pay Yourself?

Knowing how much to pay yourself is a separate topic—there's a recommended strategy for dividing your net income between yourself, taxes, and investing in the future of your company. So, let's assume you know you're able to compute the amount on your own, or with help from a CFO or your tax expert. Now you need to decide what the transaction looks like so you can get yourself that cash the *right* way.

How you pay yourself works differently for different businesses and situations. Ultimately, I recommend you consult with an accounting expert to come up with the right solution for your situation. Also, be aware that the "solution" you arrive at today may change over time as your business, situation, and the tax codes change—which is why the tax experts who work with our clients meet with us twice a year to consider whether we need to adjust the strategy for how business owners are paid.

The following are some ways that work for many business owners:

- Put yourself on payroll and give yourself a base wage, plus bonus if appropriate based on the amount you expect to be paid. For example, if your plan is to be paid between $20,000 to $30,000 each quarter based on the financial performance of the business, you might put yourself on payroll for $3,333 each half-month (totaling $20,000 in the quarter) and then give yourself a quarterly bonus to true up to the appropriate number.

- If your business is an S-Corp (or taxed as an S-Corp) and net income is over about $25,000 per year, your tax expert will likely recommend a mix of payments through payroll and distributions of profit by a direct transfer of funds or check.

- With some businesses, the owner pays him or herself regularly by taking a check directly from the company, and then works with a tax accountant at year's end to calculate the proper payroll impact to the company. For example, the owner may tell the payroll processor, "I received $X in payroll this year, but I already took it as a cash draw, so I need you to help me get the payroll records to reflect what I was intending to accomplish." Then, the payroll company essentially runs a payroll for the owner once at the end of the year. (Note: this tends to work only if you know what you're doing and why you're doing it this way.)

The strategy that's right for your business is usually going to be a blend of IRS compliance vs. tax avoidance. Most business owners won't be able to figure out what's appropriate without talking with someone who knows the rules.

Business Expenses

For many new business owners or small, one-owner businesses, there are some immediate costs that can be deducted as business expenses on tax returns right away.

Having said that, this is a good time to provide the requisite tax advice disclaimer:

I'm not a tax specialist. No one at The Numbers Edge is. Of course, we speak about tax strategy in general for situations that might apply to a lot of people, but may not apply to you specifically. There are many factors that might cause a tax strategy that works for one person not to work for another, such as whether your business runs at a profit vs. a loss; if you itemize deductions vs. take the standard deduction; if you have a lot of dependents vs. none; if you have a high income earning spouse vs. not; what state you're in, etc. Always talk to an expert in taxes who understands your situation and tax law and can provide advice. Everything related to taxes discussed in this book, on The Numbers Edge website, or by our team is intended to help you ask your tax expert good questions. We don't and can't provide definitive answers. If you need a referral to a tax expert, just ask.

For those who were W2 employees during their careers and are just now starting businesses, there probably are some costs you have carried all along that now might be considered ordinary and necessary to conducting your business.

Consider asking your tax expert whether these following are appropriate for you to consider as business expenses:

- Home internet

- Cell phone related costs

- Computer related costs

- Using your vehicle for business

- Meals for the purpose of a business meeting

- Other technology, such as tablets

- Things you buy for your office or home office (office chair, desk, printer, a lamp, etc.)

Some other costs that are considered ordinary and necessary for business have specific rules attached to them. Using logic doesn't always suffice as a litmus test. For example, wearing button-up shirts and nice dress shoes so you can look professional in front of potential clients might seem to be a logical business expense, but the IRS says otherwise. You can only expense company uniforms, not clothes that can be worn outside of business situations. In other words, if you want your dress shirts to be a business expense, you need to put the company logo on them and call them uniforms.

Here is my "go-to" test I use when deciding if I can deduct something as a business expense on my tax returns: if I were being grilled about a particular expense by an IRS auditor and needed to justify why the expense was ordinary and necessary in the course of business (as covered by IRS rules), could I justify it? If not, then I know I shouldn't be calling it a business expense. It's that simple. Of course, that's not the only test I consider, but it's a good place to start.

There are some ways to mitigate taxes that are absolutely allowed, but walking the fine line between compliance and minimizing taxes usually requires professional consultation with someone who is experienced and credentialed. As a business owner, your objective should be to pay as little taxes as possible for your situation while not crossing the line to where you would be assessed fines and penalties for making the wrong decision in the event of an audit.

Insurance

In nearly all situations, your business should have insurance. We live in a litigious society where accidents happen and unsuspecting people can be held at fault even though their intentions are good.

I know a business owner who is an above average performer. I once asked him what is it about his business approach that made him different from the others he encounters, works with, or replaces. His answer, "I cover the downside tail of the bell curve."

"What's that mean?" I asked.

Picture a bell curve of possible outcomes. On the far left are extremely unlikely scenarios, those with less than a one percent chance of happening but where consequences could potentially be devastating if they did occur. That's the tail of the left side of the bell curve. That's what insurance helps with—protecting against the unlikely, highly damaging situations by having you pay in a little bit of money regularly. Protecting against the downside tail of the bell curve, whatever that means for your business, is a highly recommended practice. It usually isn't too costly, it provides peace of mind, and it may help your company avoid going out of business.

What kind of insurance is appropriate for your business, and how much, is widely variable for different situations. That's why, as in the case with tax advice, finding someone who can give you guidance on insurance is important. But "no insurance" is likely the wrong answer.

Incidentally, protecting against the downside of the bell curve is also one of the most common reasons to create a separate legal entity for your business. For most business owners, it is uncommon to lose a lawsuit of such substantial dollar amount that you would lose the ability to keep your personal primary residence, but in rare occasions, it happens. Having a separate legal entity generally protects against this scenario when administered correctly.

BOOKKEEPING ESSENTIALS

At any company (including a brand new one), one of the first questions you need to answer is "Who will do the bookkeeping?" Someone has to, especially if the business is more than just a minor hobby.

First and foremost, appropriate bookkeeping is essential to complying with financial reporting requirements and tax returns. For most reading this book, it's a given that you need to file a tax return every year, and that return needs to reflect the income of your business activity on the appropriate forms.

Just as important, as the person in charge of the business, don't you want to have a good, updated record of the company's financial health and where its cash gets spent? (If you outright disagree with this assertion because you think it is okay to run your business without at least tracking your cash activity, you might as well stop reading right now; this book isn't for you—at least not right now. Come back when you learn from that mistake and I'll be here to support you and help you.)

Without question, I guarantee that every seasoned business owner I've met would insist that timely, accurate bookkeeping should simply be part of the recipe for operating a successful business, as important as invoicing customers or paying staff. Without timely bookkeeping, the company gets exposed to a domino effect of consequences and the manager/business owner has no financial information to understand how to improve the business performance.

Who's Keeping The Books?

Like most functions in a business, either someone is assigned responsibility for bookkeeping or it becomes the responsibility of the owner.

If the bookkeeper is you (the owner), you need at least some training in the fundamentals. It is worse to do the bookkeeping incorrectly than not to do it at all. Doing it incorrectly creates a mess that needs to be unwound, which is an exhaustive and expensive process. Perhaps worse, having wrong numbers and expecting they are accurate is like driving to a destination with a GPS that gives the wrong position. It can be better not to have the GPS at all than to have one that is inaccurate while you believe it is right.

It's shocking how many bad bookkeepers there are in the world. The good ones are naturally busy, and they aren't advertising because their schedules are full. To find a good bookkeeper, you need to ask around. Check with your tax advisor or attorney, or other acquaintances that own businesses. You're welcome to ask us if we have any referrals by emailing us at care@thenumbersedge.com.

If you're hiring a bookkeeper—either part-time or full-time—you need to know what makes a good bookkeeper vs. a lousy one. You can learn more of that here in this book and on our website www. TheNumbersEdge.com). Our bookkeeper interview questions are posted online, as is additional guidance about what you should want from your bookkeeper in terms of accuracy and how he or she can add value to the business.

Like a lot of other aspects of running a business, you want the bookkeeping (or managing the bookkeeper) to run smoothly and consistently.

For example, my rhythm working with a bookkeeper includes the following:

- Update and reconcile all bank and credit card activity weekly.

- Send me an Accounts Receivable report weekly showing who owes payment to the business.

- Send me an Accounts Payable report weekly showing who (and how much) the business owes.

- Send a transaction list weekly showing how the bookkeeper recorded all transactions since the last report, so I can look over the bookkeeping and offer any guidance or suggestions that come to mind.

- Update financial statements monthly once all invoices and similar transactions have been recorded through the last day of the month.

If interested in learning more about managing a bookkeeper, I recommend you visit www.TheNumbersEdge.com where you'll find "Course 2," which is entirely about managing a bookkeeper.

How Bookkeeping Works

In concept, the easiest form of bookkeeping—called cash basis accounting—is quite simple. There are transactions that go in and out of the company bank account, or are charged on the company credit card, and you (or the bookkeeper) utilize software to categorize each transaction as advertising, payroll, income from clients, cell phone expenses, etc. The software then groups those transactions according to purpose and allows you to run reports to show totals for each transaction type for a given time period. Easy enough, right?

The initial challenge when D-I-Y owners do their own cash basis accounting comes primarily when testing the completeness of the bookkeeping. That is, did every transaction that hit the bank account or credit card actually get recorded as its own separate transaction, and did each happen exactly once with no duplicates?

Without completeness, bookkeeping is not accurate and its value erodes quickly to potentially cause more harm than good. Luckily, there is a process that all bookkeepers use to assure completeness—it's called reconciliation (more on that later).

The accuracy of bookkeeping, particularly as a business evolves and becomes more complex, can get tricky if you don't have experience as a bookkeeper, and especially if you've not had the chance to learn from your mistakes.

A simple, new company that only has a couple of employees might record payroll cost as "staff expense" on its Income Statement. A more mature company, however, may prefer to see all of its sales and marketing expenses subtotaled together, thereby requiring that the direct labor and marketing staff be recorded differently from other employees. Then, when a company starts to acquire equipment or furniture, those acquisitions are recorded as assets (things the business owns) rather than as expenses.

As a company moves from a Level 1 business to a Level 2 business (see more on what this means in the "Leveling Up" section of the introduction), the timing of cash transactions in the company tends to lag behind actual operations. For example, you might have had to rent equipment to fulfill a commitment to a customer in August, but the equipment vendor didn't make you pay the bill until October; or you completed work with a customer in February and earned the revenue, but you allowed the client to delay payment for 30 days. The "fix" for this in your financials is to move the company from **cash basis** to **accrual basis** accounting.

In accrual basis accounting, the bookkeeping and financial statements of the business reflect the real-world timing of operations (when the company actually earns revenue from customers vs. when it gets collected, or when the company actually incurs an expense vs. pays for it).

The object of accrual basis accounting is to create two separate stories about the business:

1. What was the profitability of the company based on how the business was operated in a given period of time?

2. How is the cash impact of business activities different from the profitability calculation?

Moving the company from cash basis to accrual basis and maintaining the bookkeeping on an accrual basis should only be done by someone trained and experienced in accounting. This isn't a do-it-yourself task.

Word to the wise: as you start your company, it's best to get the bookkeeping right while your company is still small. As with many aspects of running a business, it's best to get the rhythm in place early on so it simply becomes part of "what you do."

The Importance Of Source Documents

At its core, bookkeeping is logic oriented. There is little interpretation or judgment involved with the basics of bookkeeping for a small business. The rules to follow revolve around getting every transaction right, one at a time. Knowing whether each transaction is right depends on one thing: is it supported by a source document, such as a receipt, vendor invoice, contract, lease, or something similar?

All transactions recorded in an accounting system should be based on a source or supporting reference. For example:

- Recording a meals expense at a restaurant should be based on a receipt that shows the date, location, dollar amount, and purpose of the business meeting held there.

- A customer invoice should be based on a service record, employee time sheet, a signed quote, or sales order.

- A credit memo providing a refund to a customer should be based on a written approval from the appropriate manager in the business.

- A vendor bill entered into the accounting system should reflect the vendor name, amount, invoice number, and due date that actually appear on the physical vendor bill as it was received. If an actual vendor bill was never received, then a vendor bill should not be entered into the accounting system.

For small businesses, a common inaccuracy I see related to a lack of source documents is when a company moves into a new office and records rent based on the cash outflow (which often includes a deposit and/or last month's rent) rather than what the lease says. The lease will specify what the rent should be and what the deposit should be. A deposit is like a receivable, so it needs to be on the Balance Sheet— it is something the company owns (the right to get that money back). This way you don't miss that it needs to be returned. If you expense it when you pay it, you lose the ability to track that that the landlord owes you money!

Think of it this way: source documents are akin to a paper trail of evidence that a transaction actually occurred. They are critical to having credible, accurate accounting, which is the foundation to managing your business by numbers. Most of the time, source documents will be receipts. Keep all receipts from your business expenses. Have a method to organize them and store them efficiently.

Fortunately, most good accountants and bookkeepers have ingrained in the way they go about their business the guiding principle that good accounting isn't just about getting the accounting right in the software—good accounting also needs to include leaving a trail that connects the accounting to reliable documentation so that another good accountant, if need be, could verify that the original accounting was done correctly.

The Critical Importance Of A Consistent Routine

When it comes to accounting, one key factor that leads your company to having either success or failure revolves around the accuracy of your bookkeeping. Is it both timely and recorded correctly? Both areas are prerequisites for understanding the financial health of your business. At the heart of that accuracy is your ability—and/or your bookkeeper's—to maintain a diligent routine.

Daily Routines

The best accountants "do the daily work daily." It's the ideal way to run accounting at all companies regardless of who is doing the work. If you're the owner of a business and you're also the bookkeeper, this makes you the "accountant" for your company. Doing the daily work daily means entering every bank transaction, every credit card transaction, every payable, and every customer invoice each day so the accounting is always up-to-date and running in real time.

While the benefits of such a daily routine are many, the primary one is that any of your challenging transactions get attended to quickly before they are distant memories or research projects. Businesses that update their accounting less frequently often forget why there was a particular charge on the debit card from the beginning of the previous month. As a result, they end up spending extra time hunting down the backup for the transaction (or worse, it gets permanently neglected).

For businesses that are tight on cash, maintaining an accurate, real-time cash balance in the accounting software is critical. A properly maintained accounting system knows the available cash better than the bank account does because the accounting system should know everything that has hit the bank account PLUS what the bank account doesn't already know (such as checks printed that haven't cleared yet). Thus, the true cash balance is the reconciled software balance (called the "book balance"), not the online bank account balance (called the "bank balance").

Maintaining a shorter, more frequent routine at the beginning of a new accounting process is critically important so that steps become commonplace and familiar rather than foreign and frustrating. For example, if you're reconciling only monthly, you get just one chance a month to practice it. But when reconciling daily to the online balance, you get more practice in a month (20-plus times) than most people get in a year (12 times, or once at the end of each month).

With daily routines, you quickly become a master of the task, which also sets up the D-I-Y business owner/bookkeeper to be a more effective supervisor of the bookkeeper when the company eventually hires one.

Weekly Routines

Every business should have a consistent routine of looking over certain numbers every week:

- **Who You Owe** (Accounts Payable)—Look over who you owe and pay the bills that are due in the next 10 days or so. A once-a-week check run is recommended more than an "anytime the check needs to be printed" routine.

- **Who Owes You** (Accounts Receivable)—Look at who owes you, when those payments are due, and whether any of your customers need a phone call or email reminding them to get their payment in.

- **Forecast the Future Cash Balance**—There are multiple ways to forecast what cash you expect to go in and out of the business on a weekly basis, whether you do it on the back of a napkin or simply update your multi-week cash flow forecast. Whatever your preference, your cash forecasting cadence should be weekly. We offer online tutorials and the Excel models we use with clients on our website at www.TheNumbersEdge.com or you can contact us at care@ thenumbersedge.com for more information.

Monthly Routines

Once the month ends, well-run businesses go through a process of confirming that the prior month's accounting is complete. They make any final adjustments and consider how that month's performance went compared to expectations.

For small, simple businesses with an owner who does everything, there may be no adjustments to make—the accounting is simply the result of putting every bank and credit card transaction in the system. For complex businesses that value the benefits of accrual-basis accounting, there are many standard once-a-month adjustments to make after all of the cash and card transactions have been entered.

Accounting is supposed to be something that runs lightly in the background rather than sucking up big chunks of time. Like most routine tasks, do a little each day and you'll gain confidence in that area of your business, plus the benefits will be many. Neglect the bookkeeping and you'll lose an all-important edge in managing your business.

Part of being consistent is painstakingly recording the same transactions in your accounting system the same way every day, week, or month. For example, if you pay a monthly cost for your cell phone, you don't want to one month categorize it under "Telephone Expenses" and the next under "Utilities." Keep a simple list in Excel or Evernote of recurring transactions that hit your bank account or credit card and the default account for each of those types of transactions. You'll be glad you did!

For more information about establishing and maintaining a consistent routine, download the Daily/Weekly/Monthly checklist template from TheNumbersEdge.com.

Reconciliation – The Cornerstone of Bookkeeping

I have a confession. I don't like the word reconciliation . . . and I'm an accountant. Go figure! I can only imagine, then, that if you are a business owner responsible for your own bookkeeping, the word must sound absolutely horrible to you. Nevertheless, reconciliation is the word we've been given, so use it we must.

Reconciliation is an essential tool for managing your bookkeeping. Competent bookkeepers know reconciliation frontwards and backwards. If you're not that familiar with bookkeeping and you're responsible for doing it, then you must learn what reconciliation is and how to do it. That said, let's talk about what it is, why it's so important, and how to do it.

When you think of reconciliation, think back to the good old days when you carried a checkbook and a log of your checks—a register— to keep track of the difference between what was actually in your bank account and what was on the bank statement. Essentially, you wanted to reconcile both so that, at any given time, you knew where you stood. If you wrote a check from your checkbook, you noted it in the register. Your actual bank account would reflect the transaction only once it cleared.

Fast forward to today and, for example, if I print a check from QuickBooks and give it to a vendor as payment, it doesn't clear the bank to be reflected in my account instantaneously. QuickBooks may know to deduct the amount from my account, but the bank account is not yet privy to that information. This is what accountants call a "reconciling item"—an item that's in the accounting system but hasn't yet cleared the bank account.

The important part about reconciling is that you want to be able to rely on your accounting system to provide an accurate, reliable cash balance more than you want to rely on your online banking. If you rely on your online banking balance, you're going to miss those times when you've written checks that haven't cleared—and that can easily lead to overdraft fees, bounced checks, embarrassment, or worse when you're low on cash.

Essentially, you always want QuickBooks to reflect what you know is the amount of money remaining after all of your checks have cleared, even if they haven't cleared yet.

Word to the wise: traditionally, businesses reconcile their accounting systems to their bank statements at the end of each month when they get statements. You don't have to do that. That's a pain in the neck. It takes a long time and it feels like such a laborious accounting task. What you should do is reconcile the accounting software every day to your online balance. This is a lot easier. When you reconcile every day, there are only a few transactions to manage. If something doesn't look right, you can troubleshoot it quickly.

Pending Transactions

Pending transactions can sometimes render your online bank account kind of messy, making it tough to reconcile your actual online balance. You might have to work on a one-day or two-day lag so that when you're reconciling today, you do it through yesterday's balance or the balance of the day before.

Reconciliation Is Not Optional

There are few guarantees in life, but I have one for you: if you don't keep your books reconciled you will have problems.

Failing to reconcile your accounts means you'll not only be frustrated by not knowing how much money you really have to work with, but you can end up with a tax problem at the end of the year because you won't be able to prove whether the bank transactions in your accounting system really are "complete and exact" compared to what's reflected on your bank statement.

One of the first questions your tax accountant—or anybody you might talk with about your accounting—should ask is: "Can you convince me that you've reconciled your bank statement to your accounting system so that I know all the transactions are there somewhere?"

Have I driven this point home thoroughly enough? Reconciliation isn't optional, and the more frequently you do it the easier it'll be.

More information about reconciling, including the exact steps to reconcile using QuickBooks or other accounting software, is widely available online and can be found easily through a Google search.

Doing It All (Not Just the Easy Ones)

Every business has a tricky, unusual transaction every once in a while, such as a loan payment that combines principal and interest, or a partial payment on a disputed customer bill. Those businesses with good bookkeeping identify those unusual items and consider it unacceptable to leave them "unfinished" in the accounting.

A big part of why I started the consulting company Precision Financial (www.PrecisionF.com) and the CFO membership program at The Numbers Edge is to give business owners an occasional, inexpensive sounding board to turn to when they hit those few unusual transactions and need some guidance on how to handle them. A 30-minute phone call with a CFO once a month, for some businesses, can make the difference between solid financial management and sub-par bookkeeping.

Every business owner can benefit from a best friend CFO or accountant, or someone who occasionally checks over the books to keep it 100 percent "on the rails." In my experience, if the accounting is only 95 percent right every month, in a year it will be a shaky foundation on which to understand the financial health of the business. Experienced business managers make it part of the standard process to get every single transaction recorded properly, not just the easy ones.

Every time a transaction isn't recorded completely and properly, the precision of the company accounting gets slightly more derailed. Over a long period, having to fix too many incorrect transactions can become a financial or time-consuming problem. Set your standard to get every transaction correct the first time.

Word to the wise: get every transaction right in your bookkeeping the first time. Some entries will be easy; some you won't know how to record without asking someone else (such as your tax accountant or a friend who is a CFO). Don't neglect the tough transactions. Get every one right so you never need to come back to it, and so there will never be a long-lasting blemish on your financial statements should you put it in the wrong place.

What If My "Book Balance" Is Already A Mess?

A Book Balance is what your bank account says the balance is, plus or minus anything the bank does not know about yet. Usually, that means only uncleared checks. You want to get the Book Balance correct in your accounting system and keep it correct all the time so you can rely on that number to reflect the true balance of available cash.

If your company has been in business long enough to already have the Book Balance be "unreconciled" compared to the bank account balance, here is what you need to know:

You *need* to get your accounting software reconciled to your bank account balance. That's the only acceptable solution—your way of confirming that every transaction that's hit the bank account is in the accounting system. To do this, you have to go through the reconciliation process. If there are any transactions you discover while reconciling that hit your bank but aren't in your accounting system, one at a time, you need to add them in.

Once you've done this, you might find there are more transactions in the accounting system than should be there. Common examples are checks written long ago that you know are never going to clear, or duplicate transactions that somehow got entered more than once.

No matter the reason, you've got to get these entries out of there. For some, doing so can be a little tricky, so I'm not going to get into detail here on exact steps, because exact steps are unique to each situation. As a general rule, you're often going to void these transactions in the accounting system.

This approach of voiding transactions, however, can cause challenges when you've already prepared a tax return for the year (as a general rule, you really shouldn't be changing the history for any year where you've already done a tax return). My advice is to use Google to search for what to be aware of if you need to void a prior year transaction in your accounting system—or to speak to an experienced bookkeeper. A more complex workaround may be needed to address some older transactions.

After you've gone through this process once and you've ended up with the right Book Balance, you should repeat the reconciliation process often—certainly, every month. Every week would be better, and a lot of companies do it every day.

Look at all checks that were written more than 30 days ago. Consider why they haven't cleared yet. Any deposit that you put into your accounting system that you took to the bank more than three or four days ago should have shown up on the bank statement by now. Ask yourself why a particular check might not have cleared. Keep the uncleared list minimal, so that the Book Balance becomes a reliable number by which to manage your company.

PART TWO

"As much as you need to know your operations, if you don't understand the finance side and how to do the business, you're never going to be successful. I'm successful because I know the finance side, but I also know operations; it's not an accident."
- Tilman J. Fertitta

FINANCIAL STATEMENTS

The financial statements of a business are reports that summarize the activity that was originally input, one transaction at a time, during the bookkeeping process. Reading financial statements and analyzing them is the cornerstone to managing a business by numbers successfully.

The primary financial statements of a business consist of the Income Statement, the Balance Sheet, and Statement of Cash Flows.

For many entrepreneurs, analyzing anything does not come naturally. Gaining experience involves taking what once seemed difficult and understanding it well enough to be able to teach it to someone else. All entrepreneurs need to understand the basics, so in this section we'll take a look at those basics in more detail.

For purposes of our discussion, the term "financial statements" does not refer to tax returns or to GAAP-compliant financial reports that get filed with the SEC. Instead, we're talking about financial statements that help the managers of a business run the business.

Financial statements need to be presented in ways that are both relevant and logical to business managers while still following standard accounting practices. They also need to be prepared on-time every month. Fortunately, general guidelines for reporting and preparing these statements exist for all businesses, so there's no need to reinvent the wheel.

Income Statement (Profit & Loss)

The Income Statement, also known as the Profit & Loss (P&L) Statement, shows the change in the financial health of a business for a selected period of time (usually referred to simply as the period).

The period of a P&L statement is most commonly monthly, quarterly, or annually—though in some cases the period can be weekly, daily, or some other timeframe unique to the business.

A typical Income Statement contains the following elements.

Revenue

Revenue is the money earned from customers at the time the business has fulfilled its obligation to have the right to collect it from them, regardless of whether it has invoiced the customer or actually collected the cash during that time. This concept of the timing difference between when revenue is earned compared to when it is collected in cash is particularly important to accrual basis accounting.

Under accrual basis accounting, Revenue is to be reported as follows:

1. In the period during which the company earns the Revenue by doing the work, without the influence of whether the customer prepaid for the work months in advance or whether the customer paid at the time of delivery or whether the customer paid months later; and

2. When there are direct costs (or Cost of Goods Sold) associated with fulfilling an obligation to a client, the Revenue should be recorded in the same period as that

cost. This way Revenue and direct costs always stay together, which becomes very important when analyzing and understanding the profitability of the company.

Cost of Goods Sold

Cost of Goods Sold (COGS) is the term used to reflect the direct costs of fulfilling a customer transaction. It does not include any costs associated with sales or marketing to directly acquire that customer.

For example, the Cost of Goods Sold includes the materials and labor needed to earn the Revenue from a given transaction, but does not include a sales commission paid to a salesperson for that transaction because that is considered a cost of selling the goods (the reasoning is the company might have been able to spend the same money on advertising rather than a sales commission to attract the same customer). Even in service industries where there are no direct materials and the direct costs to earn Revenue are from labor, the term Cost of Goods Sold is used still, even though the sale isn't actually of a tangible good or item.

COGS is a variable cost at a company, which means that the costs generally increase and decrease in relative proportion to the amount of Revenue. The Cost of Goods Sold does not include costs that are fixed and are not directly related to customer fulfillment, such as rent, office worker salaries, or office supplies.

Gross Profit & Gross Profit Margin

Gross Profit is Revenue minus the Cost of Goods Sold. It is reported in dollars. This is the amount of money remaining from each sale, after paying for the direct costs of the sale, that is available to go towards:

1. Selling, marketing, and promotional expenses

2. Overhead

3. Net income

Gross Profit shows the profit a company makes after covering the expenses required to provide a product or service, but before paying for the infrastructure of the business or the costs of attracting customers to that product or service.

Gross Profit Margin is Gross Profit divided by Revenue, reported as a percentage.

For example:

Revenue	$100
Cost of Goods Sold	$30
Gross Profit	$70
Gross Profit Margin	70%

For many CEOs and CFOs, Gross Profit Margin is the most important metric they track. Gross Profit Margin indicates a measure of efficiency in a company's ability to minimize the use of labor and supplies when delivering a specific result to a customer, knowing the Gross Profit Margin helps business managers determine what can be spent on all other business costs in order to break even (no profit and no loss, exactly profit neutral). Thus, it becomes the foundation for calculating how much a company can spend on other costs to reach a targeted level of profit.

A higher Gross Profit Margin is always preferable but is not always attainable depending on the industry, pricing strategy, and competition. Gross Profit Margin can be improved by increasing prices and/or decreasing the Cost of Goods Sold relative to each dollar of Revenue.

Selling, General & Administrative (SG&A) Expenses

SG&A expenses refer to all of the costs associated with acquiring customers and operating the infrastructure of a business. These costs generally are more fixed than variable, though sometimes costs to acquire a customer are variable and associated with each specific sale. When that's the case, the costs for sales or marketing would still go into SG&A expense rather than Cost of Goods Sold, even though they do vary proportionally to Revenue.

SG&A Expense is also referred to as Operating Expense or Overhead.

At companies that spend money on sales and marketing, all combined costs of sales and marketing on the Income Statement should be grouped and subtotaled, and expressed both in dollars and as a percentage of Revenue, so that business managers can consider what percentage of Revenue they're spending to acquire customers and whether that spending is providing the desired return on investment.

Net Operating Income (NOI)

NOI is the profit the company earns from operating the business. This is similar to, but not the same as, bottom line Net Income because a company may have had events affect its Net Income that are outside of its core operations. In these cases, the event and related transactions and dollar amounts should not impact reported Net Operating Income. For example:

- If a company sold a vehicle or piece of equipment, doing so may have generated a gain or a loss depending on the selling price. Unless the company is in the regular business of selling equipment, this transaction should not impact reported Net Operating Income.

- Any one-time, non-recurring unusual situation, such as the cost of a lawsuit or the gain from an insurance settlement, should not impact reported Net Operating Income.

- Interest expense is a cost associated with financing the business, not operating the business, so interest expense should not impact the reported Net Operating Income. (To illustrate, let's look at two identical businesses that operate the same way. Business A has no debt because it was backed by a wealthy owner at startup. Business B had to borrow money to begin operations. As a result, Business A has no interest expense, while Business B does. By keeping interest expense out of the Net Operating Income line, business managers for each company are able to analyze profit generated from operating their respective businesses regardless of how the companies are/were capitalized.)

- An expense a tax preparer determines to be tax deductible but that was really incurred more for the convenience of the owner vs. being a true business expense should not be included in the Net Operating Income calculation. Doing so could give those reviewing a company's financial statements the impression that the operations of the business performed less favorably for the period when the cost in question was incurred.

Other Income and Expense

This category is where items such as those noted above in the Net Operating Income discussion are added. This line item goes below the Net Operating Income line and above the Net Income line.

Net Income

The Net Income line reports the bottom-line profit of the company. Let's use a simple example to illustrate:

Revenue	$100
Cost of Goods Sold	$30
Gross Profit (Revenue minus COGS)	$70
Gross Profit Margin	70%
SG&A Expense: Selling & Marketing	$15
SG&A Expense: General & Administrative	$30
Net Operating Income (Gross Profit - SG&A)	$25
Other Expenses	$5
Net Income (NOI minus Other Expenses)	$20

Balance Sheet

The Balance Sheet shows the financial health of the business as of an exact point in time. A Balance Sheet contains three sections:

- Assets (what the business owns)

- Liabilities (what the business owes)

- Equity (the difference between Assets and Liabilities).

Assets

Many businesses own things such as:

- Cash

- Accounts Receivable (the legal right to collect money from customers where the business has already fulfilled its obligation to the customer)

- Inventory

- Equipment

- The right to use, or sometimes to obtain a refund on, certain items the business paid for in advance (for example, paying an annual insurance policy at the beginning of the year).

These are all subcategories on the Asset side of the Balance Sheet.

Liabilities

Many businesses show the following as liabilities:

- Vendor balances owed (Accounts Payable)

- Credit card balances

- Loans from banks or other lenders

- Deposits that customers have prepaid to the business in advance, but where the business has not completed its obligation to earn that revenue yet.

Similar to how Assets are handled on the Balance Sheet, the above all show up as subcategories on the Liabilities side of the Balance Sheet.

Equity

As its own separate entity, with its own financial health and its own recipe for existence, one of the truest and most important measures of the overall financial health of any business is the extent to which "what the business owns" exceeds "what the business owes." That's Equity on the Balance Sheet. When a business does not have enough assets to cover its debts (Negative Equity), it is considered insolvent.

Any bank considering whether to lend to a business is going to look immediately at the amount of Equity in the company as one of its key considerations for approving the loan or not, and at what rates or terms. A business with no Equity or Negative Equity will have a hard time getting traditional bank financing for obvious reasons: Negative Equity indicates the company has not been able to earn and retain a profit, which makes the company a risky borrower. As a business owner, you should be just as interested in seeing positive Equity in your business as a bank is.

Equity is a reflection of safety—of a company's ability to weather unfavorable events that could put a company without assets adequate to cover its debts out of business. While the importance of Equity in a business is tough to overemphasize, it's almost always underappreciated by business managers who are not experienced in business finances.

Equity and how it is trending at your business should always be something you/your business managers look at when reviewing the monthly finances.

If a company wants to increase Equity, these are the only ways to do it:

- Earn a profit and leave that money in the business rather than distributing it to the owner. (Using profits to pay down loans neither increases or reduces Equity, because that reduces both cash, an asset, and the loan, a liability, in a 1:1 ratio).

- The owner contributes capital to the company (not loaning money to the company). This increases cash in the company (an asset) without changing liabilities, thereby increasing Equity.

Current Ratio

Within both the Assets and Liabilities categories on the Balance Sheet, there are two general sub-categories: Current and Long-Term.

- Current Assets are those assets that will turn in to cash in the next year. This includes cash, Accounts Receivable, inventory, and prepayments to vendors for expenses that the company will incur in the next year.

- Current Liabilities are those liabilities that will need to be paid in cash in the next year. This includes the portion of loan principal that is required to be paid in the next year, Accounts Payable balances to vendors, prepayments from customers that would need to be refunded if the business failed to fulfill its obligations, and credit card liability.

- Long-Term Assets and Long-Term Liabilities are those items that will not impact cash in the next year.

A company always wants its Current Assets to exceed Current Liabilities. When Current Liabilities exceed Current Assets, this is an indication the company may not be able to meet its obligations in the next year, which is a serious concern.

A well-known metric applied to the Balance Sheet in nearly all industries is called the Current Ratio, which is Current Assets divided by Current Liabilities. What is considered a healthy Current Ratio for a business varies by industry. For example, a business that accepts a lot of prepayments from customers (deferred revenue liability) might have a hard time building a high Current Ratio. Regardless of industry, the low end of a healthy Current Ratio is at least 1.5:1 as a general rule, which would mean that Current Assets are 150 percent of Current Liabilities. If a company's Balance Sheet doesn't contain significant deferred revenue, a Current Ratio of 3:1 would be indicative of strong financial health.

For Level 3 and Level 4 businesses (see my definitions of business levels in the "Leveling Up" section of the introduction), the Balance Sheet is a more important measure of the financial health of the company than any other individual report.

Statement Of Cash Flows

When the accounting at a company is working correctly, transactions are being recorded regularly to both the Income Statement and the Balance Sheet using accrual basis accounting.

For example, under cash basis accounting when the company pays an attorney's bill it records the cost to legal expense at the time the check is printed. Under accrual basis accounting, when the company uses its attorney, the expense gets recorded in the period (month) in which the service was used, regardless of whether the business prepaid the attorney or actually paid the attorney months later. Under accrual basis accounting, when using a particular service but not paying for it at that time, the company records both the expense and a liability (because the company now owes the attorney). In this situation, the change in net income on the Income Statement from month to month does not necessarily represent the change in cash in the company.

The Statement of Cash Flows is an analysis that explains the differences between Net Income reported at the bottom of the Income Statement and the change in cash in the bank account.

The purpose of an accrual basis Income Statement is to explain the profitability of a company in the period in which the company operated, which can be very different from the time in which cash actually went in and out.

For example:

- We might have earned revenue from a major customer but agreed that the customer doesn't need to pay for another month.

- We might have paid all 12 months of an annual insurance policy in January, but we're really using the policy over all of the months of the year equally and could request a refund for the unused portion any time we want to cancel it.

- On the Income Statement we have a depreciation expense each month on equipment we have purchased for the business, but the cash impact already happened at the time of purchase.

The Statement of Cash Flows is designed to explain these differences, starting with Net Income at the top and concluding with the change in the company's cash at the bottom.

The Statement of Cash Flows also has few "bonus" pieces of information that you can't easily find elsewhere:

- The total amount (in a year-to-date column) you've spent on fixed assets this year

- The change in cash to draw from or repay the principal on loans

- The month-by-month distributions to owners (if the columns on your report are months).

Every Level 3 and Level 4 business owner/manager should be receiving a Statement of Cash Flows as part of his or her monthly financial reporting.

Timeliness

Financial statements provide the foundation upon which companies make critical decisions, often to get the company out of losing situations or to take advantage of opportunities. When the financial statements aren't provided on a regular, timely basis (such as within the first two weeks of the month following the reporting period), too much time can elapse, making the information outdated and less useful to decision makers. Timely financial reporting can also reflect the extent to which the accounting department operates efficiently, follows standard operating procedures, and is able to plan.

There are always reasons why accountants think financial statements cannot be delivered faster. I've heard every reason in the book. However, it can be done—and it's relatively easy when all of the accounting work is maintained in real time every day.

In a well-run accounting department, particularly for Level 2 and larger businesses, every accounting task should be completed on the earliest day it can possibly be done. Every Accounts Payable transaction should be entered in a timely manner; every bank and credit card transaction should be entered through the day prior. "Doing the daily work daily" is foundational to running accounting like an efficient factory. Accounting is supposed to be consistent, boring, and done on time!

There are many resources available online covering how to accelerate the monthly accounting process and the many benefits of timely financial statement delivery. A few minutes on Google should point you in the right direction.

How To Read Financial Statements

I'm amazed that many small business owners I meet don't read the financial statements for their companies. These are the top two reasons why:

1. Their bookkeepers or accountants simply don't produce monthly financial statements. In my experience, when business owners hire others to do the bookkeeping, monthly Balance Sheets and Income Statement at the very least should be required! In addition to their value in helping owners manage their businesses, the availability of these reports signifies the bookkeepers/accountants are actually maintaining the books and are done with the month's numbers. Good bookkeepers or accountants should have no problem incorporating monthly and timely financial statements into their deliverables, whether requested or not!

2. The business owner doesn't know how to read a financial statement.

If reason #2 applies to you, don't let it be a barrier. You can learn how to read financial statements, but it takes practice. Let's take a look at some of the elements of financial statements and how they should be presented. This will make them easier to read and understand.

Income Statement (P&L)

What does your company's Income Statement look like when you read it each month? What should it look like? What are the columns on the page? What are the rows? Is it one page long, or many pages?

Presentation formats can vary from business to business, but there is one constant that must remain: any Income Statement must allow you to compare actual results to your expectations for the period. Expectations can be based on your planned budget or based on historical data (more on this in a minute).

Why is this so important? If you have no idea what your revenue and expense expectations are for the period, it's virtually impossible to determine if the Income Statement is telling you whether your company performed well or poorly.

For example, if I reported that your company spent $3,000 on office supplies last month, would you know whether that was good or bad? Now, if I also reported what you expected to pay for office supplies last month, based on your planned budget, you would be able to compare actual costs to expected costs. In this way, you would be able to determine with ease that if your company expected to spend $7,000/month on office supplies and you spent only $3,000, then performance in this area was great, whereas if you expected to spend $500/month on office supplies, then performance was terrible.

Let's look at two ways to come up with the numbers necessary to fill the "expectations" bucket on a typical Income Statement.

1. Compared to Plan—A plan is often referred to as a "budget" or a "forecast," but I prefer to think of it as a plan. You should have a plan for what you expect will happen financially at your company each month for the next few months (or the next year). Your plan should look just like your Income Statement, so that it is easy to compare actual performance to planned performance.

2. Compared to History—I never look at an Income

Statement that only has one column for Current Month. Even an Income Statement with two columns, one for Current Month and one for Year-to-Date isn't that helpful. I want to see multiple months of history leading up to the Current Month for comparison. That sets my expectations for the Current Month.

Of course, the "home run" is to have both History and Plan on one page. My favorite Income Statement format has, as columns from left to right, the following:

- Three months of history leading up to the Current Month

- Current Month Actual, Plan, and Variance from Plan columns

- Year-to-Date Actual, Plan, and Variance from Plan columns

- The next two months of Plan performance.

Yes, that's 11 columns of information—13 if you want to add Variance Percentage—covering a 6-month span of time starting four months ago and looking ahead two.

There aren't any accounting systems that will produce this format of report by default. Don't let that be a roadblock. Your first goal is to have the best information to understand your finances available in a way that gives you an edge to accomplish your goals. Your second goal is efficiency and automation.

For a Level 1 business, just getting a monthly Income Statement to the CEO for the first time can be a huge accomplishment. The best you're probably going to be able to do initially is to create a report that depicts months in columns, showing history leading up to the Current Month. I like to see 13 months of history at most businesses, all as columns on one page. That way I can see what the company's performance was in the same period last year, plus all of the months in-between and the most recent month.

As for what gets plugged into the rows down the side of the report . . . that depends. I like generating two separate Income Statement reports, one a Condensed Summary, the other a Full Detail Version (naturally, the formats of each report and the information they contain differ).

- Condensed Summary—As the name suggests, this is a summary level Income Statement. It should fit entirely on one page so that the full story of the month for both Revenue and Net Income can be seen with one look. It should show the P&L subtotals according to expense category (personnel, facilities, outside services, travel, office costs, etc.), revealing the high-level story of how the company's finances are trending.

- Full Detail Version—This version of the Income Statement is often multiple pages and it shows every single line item from the chart of accounts. In this case, multiple pages is OK. That's because you already have a summary version that fits on one page (see above). The detailed version should have subtotals after each of the expense categories that tie to the numbers on the P&L condensed summary. (For example, wages + payroll taxes + benefits should sum to the subtotal for Personnel Costs; while rent + utilities + maintenance should sum to the subtotal for Facilities Costs, and so on). While a full detail income statement contains too much information to provide a concise picture of the overall financial health of the company, it does let you drill down on spending as well as ask insightful questions about how the accounting works at the business.

Most often, I group and subtotal expenses in the chart of accounts by the following categories, usually in this order:

- Sales & Marketing

- Personnel

- Facilities

- Professional Services

- Office Expenses or Corporate Expenses

- Travel

- Other

Balance Sheet & Statement Of Cash Flows

Similar to the Income Statement, I always want to see the Balance Sheet and Statement of Cash Flows compared to expectations. In most situations, the only expectations I can base my analysis on are the historical Balance Sheets from prior months.

As with the Income Statement, I prefer depicting 13 months as columns to show the same month a year ago, plus the most recent month, and each month in-between. What I'm looking for with the Balance Sheet is to understand which lines have improved or deteriorated over time. On the Statement of Cash Flows, I usually see significant fluctuations in the numbers for Receivables and Payables, so I'm looking for the numbers on those lines to average out near zero over time. I always include a Year-To-Date total to the right on the Statement of Cash Flows.

QuickBooks won't provide a Statement of Cash Flows with months as columns. That's frustrating. For companies that have a bookkeeper preparing a financial reporting package by exporting QuickBooks reports to Excel, it is relatively easy to build a Statement of Cash Flows into the Excel spreadsheet using formulas that won't change from month to month. At businesses that simply print their financial statements out of QuickBooks, the best you can do is output (1) a one-month Statement of Cash Flows from QuickBooks, plus (2) a year-to-date Statement of Cash Flows from QuickBooks as a separate page.

Getting Started—Just Ask "Why?"

Let's assume you're getting financial statements in the format I described over the last few pages but you have no idea what to do with them. Here's the easiest way to get started:

- Print out your pages.

- Grab a red pen.

- Pour a cup of coffee.

- Review the pages top-to-bottom, from the most recent period (which should be on the right side of the page) first.

- Look carefully at each number, and ask yourself "Why is that the number that's here?"

- Any time you're lacking confidence about the "why" of your number, circle it (make a note on the side if you choose).

That wasn't too hard, was it? Now you have some numbers and notes to refer to when you ask your bookkeeper or head of accounting for explanations. Some of your questions might sound like the following:

- "Office supplies were $650 last month? Why? What caused that? What did we buy?"

- "Gross profit margin went from 31 percent to 33 percent? Why?"

- "Revenue increased by $20,000 compared to last month. Why? What did we sell more of, and to whom?"

- "On my Balance Sheet, it says I have Accounts Receivable of $22,500? Why? What makes up that balance?"

- "I had Positive Net Income last month on my Income Statement, yet my bank account went down. Why?"

The answer to the "why" part of each question typically lies in either your accounting system transaction list or can be explained (possibly requiring research) by your bookkeeper or accountant.

P x Q

As I mentioned earlier, Gross Profit Margin is possibly the most important component of a business's finances to understand. Initially, wrapping your mind around the number and what it really means for your company might be a bit of a challenge.

Chances are your accountant or bookkeeper has been giving you an Income Statement with your entire business blended into a single Gross Profit line. Now, if you own a business that provides multiple types of services to multiple customers using multiple direct labor staffs, how can you tell which service offerings are positively vs. negatively influencing your Gross Margin? Or if you sell multiple products, which products are at higher margins vs. lower ones as factored in to the weighted average reported on the P&L? You can see how the lack of detail can make it almost impossible to discern your good performers from poor ones.

As a rule, you should always understand your profitability and your Gross Margin at the most specific levels possible: by revenue stream, by customer, by employee, by job, by SKU if you sell units of goods, etc. Your company margin is equal to the sum of your margin on each of these building blocks.

How you can best report and use this information likely will need some tailoring depending on the particular business you're in. But know this: every business can break down how it earns its margin and then use that information to increase profit by treating lower performers differently from the all-stars.

Revenue is always made up of what I call "P times Q." P is the price you sell something for. Q is the quantity of sales. If you know your Ps and your Qs, you will be more profitable than if you don't.

To illustrate, let's look at an example from my past.

Some years ago, I was engaged to be the CFO at a company providing professional services to larger companies. This typically entailed large projects ranging anywhere from $50,000 to $2 million apiece. The company was profitable, and the management team received and read monthly financial statements. Unfortunately, those financial statements were not insightful enough to help management know how to act to improve performance.

Since the employees tracked their hours in a timekeeping system, we could track every hour worked on every project. Based on the fully burdened cost of each employee, we knew what each hour was costing us. Similarly, based on the sales price we quoted for each project compared to the expected hours, we knew what we should be earning for each hour worked on said project.

Once we implemented tracking of our margin at a level deeper than just the summary level Income Statement, we discovered that some employees were highly profitable while others were being sold at too low an hourly rate compared to what they were actually costing us. This was due to a combination of poor pricing and some employees simply not working enough client hours to bring their salaried costs down to the expected costs on an hourly basis.

Armed with this new insight, we researched whether any pricing and performance issues were being caused by the "P"—whether we were pricing each person's hours appropriately to the customer—or the "Q," knowing that if the employees were fully utilized on client work the hourly price would be right, but that if they were not fully utilized, the hours would be too low to earn a margin on that person over the course of a week or a month.

As a result, we increased pricing in areas where we could. We also began to manage people differently and jobs more proactively to maximize everyone's time, including a weekly meeting to review each direct labor team member's client-billable hours for the prior week and to brainstorm how to deploy anyone who was underperforming on hours to other projects or assignments during down times.

The entire process of identifying the issue, implementing improvements, and realizing desired margins by employee (as compared to overall margins), took about a year. In that time, we managed to improve Gross Profit Margin at the company by nine percent on $10 million in total company annual revenue—an additional $900,000 in annual Net Income that could have been picked up years earlier if someone had only thought to look at the company's financials and margins this way.

When we started down this path, we didn't know what to measure, why we were going to measure it, or really what to do about it. Most people involved had an "if it ain't broke, don't fix it" attitude. But once we started asking "Why?" and prepared the reports and analyses necessary to answer our questions, we were able to make significant and impactful changes to the way we did business.

Key Performance Indicators (KPIs)

Price and quantity statistics are examples of Key Performance Indicators, commonly abbreviated as KPIs. A KPI is a statistical or quantitative measurement that influences the financial results of a company but are not the financial results that actually appear on an Income Statement or Balance Sheet. KPIs could be computations or calculations.

Examples of KPIs include the following:

- Number of customers

- Employee turnover ratio

- Revenue per labor hour

- Percent of phone calls answered within a certain time

- Number of business locations or franchises

- Headcount of employees

- Number of incident free workdays

- Average time to collect payment from customers

- Backlog of client work under contract

- Number of billable hours worked

- Number of overtime hours worked.

As a manager of a business, decisions in the operations of the business have an impact on the financials, but the financials themselves aren't actually the decisions that are made. Financial results are only an outcome of the decisions made.

KPIs are the statistics that business operators can manage to that are influencers or predictors of the financial outcomes.

KPIs are as important to track and report as financial statements are. They should be analyzed and correlated to the financial statement results. In well-run companies, KPIs are reported to management in the same monthly report as the financial statements, thereby making it a "management report" rather than a financial report only.

Consider this general guidance regarding KPIs:

- In any business where direct labor is important to revenue generation "direct labor utilization" should be a KPI. Utilization refers to the ratio of productive time (which means revenue-generating time) to the time that was expected to be productive. Ideally, employee utilization is measured both weekly and monthly. A target or expectation is set and each employee's utilization is identified as underperforming, on par, or overperforming. I like a simple red-yellow-green color code for each.

- One of the most important KPIs in the hotel industry is capacity—as in, "What percent of maximum capacity was filled last night, last week, or last month?" To the extent a business can identify its maximum capacity, it should establish a KPI that tracks the percentage of total capacity filled by revenue generating business.

- QuickBooks doesn't have a place to track KPIs. Some other accounting systems have an area of the chart of accounts that are designated for statistical tracking (often called the "9000 Accounts"). That said, here's a trick to use with QuickBooks that does afford some KPI tracking ability (the method isn't pretty, but it does create a way to track KPIs in a centralized software that the company already uses for bookkeeping):

— Select an area in your chart of accounts (I suggest "Other Expense") and create an account called KPIs.

— Next, create a subaccount for the KPI you want to track in QuickBooks. For this example, let's assume your business is a restaurant and the KPI to track is "Number of Guests." The subaccount would be "Guests."

— Create another account right below it, but part of the same parent-level subtotal, and give it a similar name (such as "Guests-2").

— Now, at the end of each day, week, or month (whatever the desired period is), the company bookkeeper can add up the number of guests in that period and enter a debit to the first account, "Guests," and a credit for the same amount to the second account, "Guests-2." The accounts will net to zero at the subtotal level, so will have no impact on the overall financial statement totals.

- KPIs should be reported in a trended format or compared to expectations, just as Income Statements and Balance Sheets are. For example, in service businesses that generate revenue based on hours worked, the management reports might contain graphs and tables based on the number of hours worked by month and average revenue per hour—all easy metrics for which management can establish expectations and standards. Tracking such KPIs can also help the business analyze whether revenue is appropriate on the financial statements for the number of billable hours worked by staff. When possible, these kinds of metrics (Revenue, Hours, and Revenue per Hour) should be reported by client or by project. Doing so can help confirm whether each client was invoiced appropriately, reveal if any hours were errantly left unbilled, or identify clients who have an unusually high or low revenue per billable hour calculation. This type of analysis also makes further research possible into why some numbers might vary from expectations, which in turn creates opportunities to avoid similar mistakes going forward.

Leading vs. Lagging Indicators

One of the additional reasons to track KPIs is to monitor Leading Indicators vs. Lagging Indicators.

- Leading Indicators are early predictors of the future financial health of the business.

- Lagging Indicators are measurements that reflect the financial health of a business after any decisions related to them have been made.

Unfortunately, most Level 1 businesses manage their bookkeeping on a cash basis. Cash is the ultimate Lagging Indicator. Accrual basis accounting reflects activity, through the financial statements, earlier than on a cash basis and can be used to predict changes in cash.

As an example of how cash is a Lagging Indicator, let's assume you want to increase cash in your business. In order to receive or increase cash in the business by collecting from a customer, you first need to send the customer an invoice. Of course, before you can send an invoice, you need to do the work (or deliver a product). So, doing the work is a leading indicator of what invoices are going to be sent, which is a leading indicator of receiving cash.

Now, before doing the work, you need a prospective client to become an actual customer. Before that, you might have to make a proposal. Before making the proposal, there's probably some sort of sales pitch, meeting, or presentation involved, and before the sales pitch or meeting, the potential client somehow has to enter your sales pipeline as a prospect.

Thus one of the Leading Indicators that predicts whether your business's cash balance is going to increase or decrease is the size of your sales pipeline, followed by a slew of other activities (the number of sales pitches, the number of presentations delivered, the win/loss percentage converting sales prospects into customers, the number of billable hours worked on client projects, and the dollar amount of invoices sent out)—each important in its own right and each an indicator of future performance.

What this example shows is that a business can't be managed effectively and proactively by looking only at the cash balance because that balance is often the last thing to happen (the Lagging Indicator) in a long list of situations and other KPIs affecting the business.

Breakeven Point

The Breakeven Point is particularly important to any business that does not experience an abundance in profit. It's the exact amount of revenue needed to generate zero net income—no profit and no loss.

The Breakeven Point is a function of Contribution Margin (Gross Profit minus all other variable expenses) and fixed expenses. A low Breakeven Point is preferred over a higher Breakeven Point, because a lower Breakeven Point means the minimum revenue needed to cover expenses is lower, and therefore easier to earn. A company's Breakeven Point lowers when fixed expenses decrease or when Contribution Margin as a percentage of revenue increases.

A Breakeven Point is usually stated in dollars, such as "Our Breakeven Point is $50,000 in monthly revenue," but can also be calculated in units, such as "Our breakeven point is 1,850 billable hours in a month."

To illustrate the Breakeven Point, let's assume in a given month that a company has fixed expenses of $250,000, Gross Profit Margin of 55 percent, and variable operating costs (in this case sales commissions) of 10 percent of Revenue. That means for every dollar in Revenue generated, 45 percent goes to Cost of Goods Sold.

In this example, we would say that the Contribution Margin—the amount each dollar in Revenue "contributes" towards fixed costs and profit—is 100 percent minus the 45 percent for COGS minus the 10 percent for other variable costs, or 45 percent of Revenue.

To calculate the Breakeven Point in dollars, we would then divide the fixed expenses ($250,000) by the Contribution Margin (45 percent) resulting in $555,555 in Revenue needed to break even, producing no revenue and no loss.

Now let's work the calculation backwards and prove the math:

Revenue	$555,555
Cost of Goods Sold (45% of revenue)	$250,000
Gross Profit	$305,555
Variable Costs (10% of revenue-sales comm'n)	$55,555
Contribution Margin	$250,000
Fixed Expenses	$250,000
Net Income	$0

Diving deeper into the numbers, we can now calculate our Breakeven Point in hours and units.

- If we know our business provides hourly services and our average bill rate is $150/hour, we can divide our revenue ($555,555) by the hourly rate ($150) to see that we need to bill 3,704 billable hours to break even.

- If a company sells products at $125 per unit, we can divide our revenue ($555,555) by the unit sale price ($125) so that we know we need to sell 4,444 units to break even.

A business might want to calculate the cash-basis breakeven, because the revenue needed to report zero Net Income on the Income Statement might be different than the revenue needed in order to be cash-neutral. Differences between cash and Net Income might include regular loan payments or planned distributions for the owner based on profits earned in a prior period, or to back out of the calculation that one of the costs impacting Net Income is

103

depreciation, a non-cash expense.

In such cases, adjust the fixed expenses number higher for additional cash outflows that need to be covered by the revenue earned, and reduce the fixed expenses by any non-cash costs, such as depreciation.

A business that is performing better than the Breakeven Point has a margin of safety. The margin of safety refers to the sales above the Breakeven Point. For example, if a company is currently selling 4,000 units and it has calculated that the breakeven point is 3,600 units per month, the margin of safety is 400 units, the difference between those numbers.

PART THREE

"See, when you drive home today, you've got a big windshield on the front of your car. And you've got a little bitty rearview mirror. And the reason the windshield is so large and the rearview mirror is so small is because what's happened in your past is not near as important as what's in your future."
- Joel Osteen

DRIVING OUT OF THE WINDSHIELD
(Rather Than the Rearview Mirror)

The whole point of reviewing the history of where a company is, and has come from, is to get an idea for where the company will be in the future. The past can't be changed, but the future can.

You're already ahead of much of the competition if you have a good understanding of the current financial health of your business, including which numbers and KPIs are trending favorably vs unfavorably. The great business managers use this information to build out their crystal balls of where their companies are going to be in the future, using that knowledge to make decisions.

When a business does not have a firmly instituted monthly routine of reviewing historical data and recent trends in its financial statements and KPIs, it must create one. Developing that routine and resulting reports is the first milestone. Once that process becomes firmly entrenched, the focus should then turn toward where the company is going to be in the future vs. where it has been in the past.

For starters, any forward-looking company should develop a forecast (in Excel) based on a combination of historical trends and knowledge gleaned from its business managers of what is expected to change in the next six to 18 months. The forecast should be the company's collective "latest, greatest crystal ball" of knowledge and expectations based on available information. It should be updated monthly and presented as part of the management report and monthly financial discussion process. This allows the focus of those discussions to change from where the company has been to where it is going.

- *Before*—This is how the financial health of the business has been last month, last quarter, and year-to-date.

- *After*—A month ago we discussed that at the end of this year, we project the financial health of the business to be here. Now, our latest crystal ball envisions the financial health of the business at year's end to be this. Let's discuss why our expectations changed from where they were a month ago, to include how much of that change is due to this month's actual performance varying from our original forecasts and how much is due to changes we made to our forecasts for future months.

The purpose of forecasting is to raise visibility about where the future financial health of the business is going to be for management so they can maintain the status quo (if they are pleased with the company's outlook) or make decisions sooner rather than later to affect any changes deemed necessary to improve the company's position.

Having a forecast also allows for scenario analysis. If a company's CEO were to say, "We're thinking about hiring two more members of the sales staff and we expect the impact on revenue and cost in the first three, six, and 12 months after they start to be A, B, and C," those numbers can be plugged into the company's forecast and their anticipated impact on the company's future financial health tracked at various points in time.

A Budget vs. A Forecast

One of the most common financial management practices is to build an annual budget and to measure actual performance against it. I certainly encourage the practice. However, for some small businesses, the benefit to doing so is underwhelming compared to the insistence of most finance types that "every company needs to have a budget."

Before we look at how businesses should use a budget, forecast, and historical performance data together, let's clarify how the terms "budget" and "forecast" are similar, how they differ, and how businesses should use them.

Your First Priority

For most small businesses considering whether to create a forecast or a budget, their first priority should be to develop a forecast. A forecast is the latest, updated crystal ball that reflects the company's candid expectations of where the financial health of the business is headed in the next six to 18 months. A forecast may change regularly, though the recommendation is that it be changed no more frequently than once a month and no less often than quarterly.

As a company moves through the year, reviewing actual financial information every month and updating its forecast accordingly, eventually the company approaches the end of its fiscal year. The company's attention now turns toward the performance forecast for the year ahead. It's at this point the business owner (or management team if it's a bigger company) should take an extra, deliberate look at the assumptions and expectations for the upcoming year. Does the company's forecasted position for the following year still match the company's business goals and owner's personal goals? Based on the answer, the owner or management may decide to modify the forecast slightly to emphasize any new goals or targets for the end of the coming year.

For example, the owner might say, "At the one percent per month revenue growth we've been experiencing, our current forecast reflects revenue will be 12 percent higher at the end of next year than at the end of this year. However, our objective is to grow faster than that and we're ready to dedicate more time and resources. To meet our goals, we need revenue to be 15 percent higher at the end of next year than this year. That needs to be our plan, so let's build those assumptions into next year's forecast, including everything we believe we need to do and track next year, by month, in order to hit that goal."

Your Official Plan (aka The Budget)

At the point the forecast is approved by all appropriate parties, it becomes the company's official plan for the year. Only then, once the plan is locked down for a particular period, do we call it the budget.

Invariably, within a month or two of finishing and operating under the budget, something will be off from plan. It always happens. In fact, lots of things are likely to be off from budget within a couple of months. Customer growth will be more or less than budgeted expectations, for example, or hiring may have deviated from the plan.

At many companies, by the time the following year is half over, managers might be thinking, "Everything is so different from what we budgeted, this budget is practically useless."

If this happens, don't be discouraged. Consider it an opportunity to evaluate what could have been improved in the prior year's budgeting process. Remember, a budget reflects the plan for where management at the end of last year wanted the company to be at the end of this year (such as "generating this much revenue," "having this much net income," "having this much cash on hand," and so on). Even if things don't go exactly as designed, it's still important to consider and benchmark company performance at the summary level for all key objectives, comparing where management said they wanted to be to actual results.

Changing The Forecast

Whether a company is close to the performance that was budgeted or far from it, it should maintain the forecast on a monthly basis. After the first month or two of the fiscal year, the forecast and the budget are probably the same numbers. By the third or fourth month, budgeted numbers that aren't going to be hit exactly as planned become more obvious. They should be modified based on the latest crystal ball thinking and become, once again, referred to as the latest forecast.

Each month, the person responsible for leading the process of forecasting, budgeting, and financial statements should prepare not only updated reports, but also talking points for management. A sample talking point might read like this, "We're halfway through the year. Based on the actual performance through the first half, plus our latest crystal ball (forecast) for the second half, we're expecting the total year to beat our revenue budget by 12 percent, to have a Gross Profit Margin that is in line with budget, to report SG&A expenses that are seven percent higher than budget, and to report Net Income that is 24 percent higher than budget."

I find the best way for historical information and forecasted information to be presented is together in one report. I've used what I like to call an "Actual + Forecast Report" to combine both actual/historical numbers (looking back) and forecast numbers

110

(looking ahead to future months).

Picture the report as an Income Statement, where the months are column headers across the top from January through December, with a Total Year column at the far right. For the months that actual numbers are known and complete, the historical information for each line item goes into those columns. For the months that haven't happened yet, the latest forecast numbers for each line item go in those columns. The entirety is the company's combined picture for the year.

A Word To The Wise

If you follow my forecast and budget reporting recommendations exactly as outlined here, you might generate 12 updated forecasts during the year, plus the annual budget. With all that information at your fingertips, you, the business owner, management, or all of the aforementioned might be tempted to begin analyzing every difference between each version:

- How did this month's forecast vary from the forecast presented last month . . . and why?

- How does this month's forecast vary from this month's budget . . . and why?

- How did last month's actual performance vary from the last time that month was forecasted . . . and why?

Although interesting, such analysis can be very time consuming.

Earlier in my career, in my role as a financial analyst with a private equity-owned business, part of my job was to analyze all of these variances and changes on a regular basis. It consumed about half of my job. Although there was some value in this information because it was used by very savvy investors and managers, for most companies it's just not worth it.

In my experience, it's best to keep it simple by focusing on how the company is doing against the plan (budget) and where the company is likely to go (forecast).

More Guidance On Budgeting & Forecasting

When it comes to diligently attending to historical financial information vs. forecasting or budgeting, keep in mind that looking ahead is always more valuable. A business should be managed to where it is going, not to where it has been.

As we know, business decisions most directly impact KPIs rather than the financial numbers themselves, which reflect the outcome of the events and transactions of the business. As such, the KPIs should be forecasted as well.

- If a service company is planning to make decisions that will improve labor efficiency in the next year, it should forecast an improvement in direct labor utilization from (for example) 80 percent to 83 percent, which then can drive a computed favorable impact on cost and Net Income.

- If a real estate company is forecasting to improve from an average of 15 closed transactions per month to 22 such transactions by the end of the coming year, those statistics should be forecasted along with the planned revenue per transaction.

I strongly encourage all forecasting to be prepared based on extremely candid assumptions—the genuine best estimate of what is going to happen. If a forecast needs to be provided to an external party with numbers that are more optimistic or pessimistic than candid, you can always copy the forecast to make adjustments to it and save the modified forecast with a new file name.

In general, it's not a good practice to prepare overly optimistic revenue forecasts, and then to forecast expenses based on those revenue levels. Doing so could result in overspending on expenses even though the revenue may not pan out as hoped.

If appropriate, consider referring to the budget as the company's "plan" if the term "budget" meets with resistance or hesitation. This may help non-finance minded managers at a company become more comfortable with the process.

Always budget by month. If you don't, it will be much tougher to prepare an "Actual + Forecast" report, and to explain variances between actual and budget in the prior month's performance.

Much of this book is about the way experienced business managers operate their businesses—things that first-time business owners and managers may not have learned yet. Setting expectations that a forecast, or crystal ball, is needed at all times to run the business is very important. A forecast tells you where the company is going in relation to its goals and what accomplishments need to happen along the way to reach those forecasted numbers.

For additional guidance, I invite you to visit our website at www.TheNumbersEdge.com. There you can learn more about the exact steps we use to build a forecast or budget. If you get stuck, contact us at Care@TheNumbersEdge.com. We're nerdy and love this topic and would be happy to help.

Cash Flow Forecasting

Cash flow forecasting is not the same as the forecasting we've been discussing in relation to building a budget and following a plan. Cash flow forecasting is about predicting a company's cash balance in advance, including the low cash point, so that business managers can know as far in advance as possible if or when a cash flow problem might come.

Even profitable businesses with dedicated employees and products or services loved by customers can run out of cash. Sometimes it's as simple as a couple of top customers not being able to pay their bills on time.

Businesses often go out of business because they run out of cash without having enough time to prepare for it.

- If I were to tell a business owner that the company is going to run out of cash and won't have enough money to make payroll in 10 to 12 weeks, in many circumstances, the owner would be able to come up with at least a temporary solution to extend the life of the company.

- If I were to tell that same business owner only two weeks ahead of time, most likely the company would be doomed.

Cash flow forecasting is about providing visibility about a company's cash position to the business owner/manager with as much advance notice as possible.

There are two types of cash flow forecasting recommended for any business that is less than flush with cash:

1. Short-Term Cash Flow Forecasting—This process lists every major cash inflow and outflow that is expected to happen by a certain point in time. Usually that point in time is either the end of the week or the next payroll date. The purpose is to forecast as accurately as possible how much cash the company will have on the date the next payroll needs to be funded, thereby providing a scenario analysis opportunity to say "Let's not pay these bills until after that payroll" or "We better make sure these two payments are coming in before payroll, because we need them, so let's contact those customers and ask for an update."

2. Multi-Week Cash Flow Forecasting—Also known as a Weekly Cash Flow Forecast or 13-Week Cash Flow Forecast (or as I refer to it, "The best business management tool ever invented"). This is a spreadsheet featuring weeks as columns and is designed to track expectations for all inflows and outflows of cash weekly. The goal is to calculate expected cash balances at the end of each week for many weeks to come.

At www.TheNumbersEdge.com, we provide video training on how to create and maintain both of these cash flow forecasts, including the same cash flow forecast models we use with our clients. It wouldn't be feasible to translate the video guidance and the on-screen development of the Excel models into text here. However, the importance of cash flow forecasting is critical for most small businesses. Our consulting team has seen dozens of businesses saved by implementing cash flow forecasting into their weekly routines.

When Cash Is Tight

I've worked with a lot of companies that lacked abundant cash. They were always having to decide who was the highest priority to be paid and who could be lower on the list—and many had been doing this for years.

Businesses that are habitually low on cash need a process for choosing who to pay with limited cash on hand in a way that sustains the business, and they have to get it right every week.

As a business owner with low cash reserves, your company needs a recurring process for aggregating and tracking what it owes, complete with dates and amounts due. If you use QuickBooks (or similar) and enter all vendor bills when they are known with correct due dates, then the majority of this information should come easily from your accounting system on the Accounts Payable Aging Detail or the Unpaid Bills Report. (Note: there may be times that you owe a vendor for multiple invoices, one of which was due last week, for example, and another that is not due for two more weeks. The payments owed to that vendor need to be separated because paying the first bill is a higher priority than the second bill.)

Here is one approach to creating such a weekly process:

1. Export the list of everything that your business owes to an Excel spreadsheet. Sort the information by due date with those due soonest at the top.

2. Consider what other payments you need to make and what else is owed that's not on the accounts payable list, such as loan payments or credit card payments or next month's rent. Add those manually to the Excel spreadsheet so that

it becomes a list of everything you owe in the near term.

3. Next, manually arrange the payables into the priority order for who gets paid first, second, third, and so on. Usually you can do this by inserting blank rows in the desired order and then pasting the information there.

4. Each payable should be grouped into general categories and assigned a priority, which I call "Tier 1," "Tier 2," and "Tier 3." What you should end up with are two types of prioritizing: first with every payable assigned to either Tier 1, 2, or 3, and then ordered within each tier, with the highest priority at the top.

5. On the far right of your spreadsheet, create a column called Cumulative and create a formula that adds together all of the amounts due at or above that formula. For example, on the second row of data, the formula would add together the first and the second payable amounts using a sum formula. On the fifth row, it would add together the first five payables, etc.

6. This Cumulative column allows you to see how much and which vendors you could pay up to a certain dollar amount. For example, you might determine you only have $20,000 to apply to payables this week. By looking at the Cumulative column, you can see very easily which line items add up to $20,000 so that you or your finance manager knows where to stop, paying everything before that line.

For most businesses with Accounts Payable that exceed cash available, this process is repeated every week. It is possible that in the middle of the week there are rearrangements within the list. For example, a vendor might call and say he or she is going to cut service off for an operationally critical supply until the next payment is received. In that case, you might move that vendor up the priority list for getting paid. So consider this report a living document that gets rearranged often to take into account the latest information.

Assigning Priorities

You might be wondering within the list of payments owed, how you determine which payments should be high priority vs. mid priority vs. low priority (Tier 1, 2, or 3)?

In the first tier should be anything that's mission critical to keeping your doors open, the first of which is payroll. If a company can't afford payroll and employees don't get their checks, there is typically a very small grace period before employees don't come back and continuity of business operations is jeopardized. Payroll is pretty much always going to be number one and you'll let almost any vendor go unpaid if you have to choose between paying a vendor and making payroll.

The second tier is typically a government source that is owed taxes. The IRS, state governments, and a variety of other agencies tend to have standard operating processes that make life very difficult if they don't get the taxes or other monies they're owed.

In the third tier typically go those vendors that if not paid can cut off a service or supply that results in material consequences for your business.

After that comes everyone and everything else.

With these processes in place, deciding which vendors to pay and how much becomes more of a mathematical function than an emotional consideration. Cash available goes to the highest priority payables and everyone else just needs to wait.

Tight Cash Flow Suggestions

In order to maintain a sufficient cash balance to cover payroll and other top priority expenditures, accounting and cash management procedures when the cash balance is close to zero are more involved than when cash is abundant.

These cash management procedures are suggested when there is a risk of insufficient funds:

- The bank account is to be reconciled daily. This should be done as the first task each morning.

- A daily cash report is to be distributed each morning to the appropriate members of finance and executive management. This should be done immediately after the bank account   is reconciled. (More information about what a daily cash report involves is discussed below.)

- Each customer invoice in Accounts Receivable is to be analyzed and a precise expected date for receipt of payment identified. If you are not sure about an invoice, review it carefully for the original invoice date and payment terms. If appropriate, contact the customer's accounts payable department and discuss the expected payment date with him or her.

- Accounts Payable is to be analyzed carefully. Each Accounts Payable item should be given a "target date" to send payment and assigned a grade regarding the extent to which the vendor can be stretched (and for how long).

- The "float" (or value) of uncleared checks issued but that have not cleared the bank yet is to be analyzed to determine to what extent float can be relied upon if needed. Review the recent historical float and analyze the current uncleared items to determine which are of large dollar value. These are transactions that can reduce the float substantially with a single deposit of a check to a vendor.

- Checks printed for vendors are to be approved in advance of check printing by the designated controller, CFO, business owner, or manager responsible for managing the cash balance.

- In general, holding printed checks is discouraged. The preference is not to print the check at all so that QuickBooks reflects vendor balances more accurately. If checks are to be held, then checks printed for disbursement are only to be sent to vendors upon specific approval of the designated controller, CFO, business owner, or manager responsible for managing the cash balance.

- Cash balance is to be forecasted each day through the next payroll or until another appropriate milestone, such as when a large payment clears. Any day when the cash balance/book balance could be below zero is to be brought to the attention of the designated senior finance manager immediately.

- All other sources of financing, including overdraft protection are to be identified immediately.

- The next credit card payment and amount are to be quickly assessed. Determine the minimum payment allowed to be made on the credit card and assess the consequences of paying less than the full balance.

- The weekly multi-week cash flow report must be produced on a reliable, consistent basis. The suggested practice is to publish a weekly cash flow report by mid-day Tuesday that covers actual transactions through the previous Sunday night. Every transaction forecasted in the early weeks should be specifically identified and care should be given to consider whether the dollar amount and expected week of payment are accurate. Consider involving executives or others who are not routinely involved in the cash flow forecasting process, but have insight about the timing and amount of cash transactions, to improve accuracy of the projection. As a reminder, instructions for the weekly cash flow forecast process can be found on our website, www.TheNumbersEdge.com.

- In general, the number one priority is to cover payroll. When employees don't get a paycheck on time, the negative effects on the company can be severe and long-lasting. The objective is not to let anyone get the impression that there is a low cash balance, especially regular employees.

Daily Cash Reporting

A daily cash report typically is a spreadsheet attached to an email. In general, it contains the following information:

Section One – Cash Balance

- Book Balance (this should tie in to the accounting system)

- Uncleared checks and deposits in transit, listed individually with vendor name, check date, and dollar amount

- Bank Balance (this should tie in to the bank account balance and should equal Book Balance plus uncleared checks/ deposits in transit)

Section Two – Accounts Receivable

- Accounts Receivable should be listed by invoice, including the invoice date, amount, and due date; commentary should be noted as appropriate about the expected date to receive payment.

- This should be updated daily.

Section Three – Accounts Payable

- Accounts Payable should be listed by invoice, including vendor name, invoice date, terms, due date, and amount; commentary should be noted about the flexibility of the vendor to be paid late for each item, if appropriate.

Section Four – Summary

A summary page should contain the following information:

- Bank Balance

- Uncleared checks (total)

- Book Balance

- Today's expected deposit

- The next date payroll will clear the bank account

- The amount expected to clear the bank account on the date mentioned above

- The total Accounts Payable balance over 30 days

- The total Accounts Payable balance over 60 days

- The total Accounts Receivable balance past current

- Outstanding line of credit balance

- Any other important payment or receivable items should be specifically noted in the summary (such as a large credit card or insurance payment due, etc.)

This summary page should be pasted as a picture into the body of the email for the convenience of recipients.

Lastly, and this is perhaps my most important piece of guidance regarding cash flow: when you need to cut expenses, do it fast.

Don't delay the inevitable. Even business owners who get ahead on cutting costs go through a lot of stress trying to right-size the ship and may realize they haven't done enough to save the business. Business managers who know how to cut decisively when the company needs to reduce expenses are more successful than those who hesitate and wait.

PART FOUR

"After 39 years of business, I'm still learning. I go through this every year—identifying new strategies that are extremely important."
- Fred DeLuca

STRATEGY

When a business is small and first starting out, the main goal of most owners is simply to pay themselves. At this stage, owning the business is just a job. With some luck, effort, and skill, it becomes a job that pays at least as well as other comparable jobs, but is a lot more enjoyable because with it comes flexibility, independence, and pride of business ownership.

In these small, founder-oriented businesses, additional goals usually emerge to complement the initial goal of paying the business owner:

- To accomplish the owner's personal goals, which might include a certain work-life balance or support of a particular lifestyle that allows time for family, travel, or hobbies

- To build wealth for the business owner over the long term

- To build value in the business so that it can be sold or transferred to someone else down the road.

By the time a Level 1 business becomes a Level 2 business (see definitions of business levels in the "Leveling Up" section of the introduction), these other goals often start to play roles in the strategy of the company. For example, once a business is able to pay the business owner regularly and appropriately, the next focus tends to be on longer-term wealth building using tax deferral strategies rather than simply paying profits to the owner in cash.

Establishing your own priorities and objectives as owner is one of the benefits of owning a business. Three people can all own similar businesses and have completely different objectives and definitions of success. One might be interested in funding a lavish lifestyle today, while another might be focused on reducing the number of years until enough money has been saved for retirement, while the third might sacrifice heavily today to build a company that is well-positioned to be sold in the future.

Regardless of the objective, there are many similarities in the fundamentals of business strategy—both long-term strategic and short-term tactical—that help all business owners accomplish their goals.

Playing The Long Game

A business owner should always have an eye squarely on the long term. Owning and developing a business to success takes patience and is best suited as a long-term endeavor.

I compare a business to a snowball rolling down the hill, or a building that is built one level at a time. Usually the progress starts slowly and then picks up speed over time. With a business, if you continue to put one foot in front of the other down a well-thought-out path, most of the time you'll end up in a desirable position.

My advice is to play the long game always, whatever the "long game" means to you. Sacrificing today in exchange for a higher likelihood of bigger benefits tomorrow will usually serve you well.

In business, playing the long game should involve protecting your business against risk and downside, building cash reserves and keeping debt to a reasonable level, and diversifying your customer and vendor base so that one unexpected disruption to a key component of your business doesn't bring the whole company down.

Imagine you start a small business and in a couple of years it grows to where it's bringing in $250,000/year in revenue. Now fast-forward five years and someone says to you "Your business has generated over $1 million in revenue since you started! That's great! How much of that have you been able to save?" Do you want your answer to be "Um... nothing"? Certainly not! But it will be if you don't have a plan to save a portion of the revenue that comes in.

A business that you want to succeed over the long term needs to be cared for the same way you care for a person you love. It needs to be

- Protected from risk and harm

- Developed to be better and smarter next year than it was the year before

- Free to be agile and flexible without undue constraints or burdens.

A business is delicate, which is something most of us never really understand as employees. We don't see what a business owner sees—that it needs to be insulated from attack, which requires both offensive and defensive strategies.

If you own a business and you have children, you can draw a parallel between what you want your business to become and what you desire for your children.

- You hope your children find their successful places in the world by bringing their unique qualities to society in ways that resonate successfully with others, and therefore they thrive with opportunity and success.

- You hope your children have the discipline to save some of their incomes over time, earning the flexibility that comes from having nest eggs rather than living paycheck to paycheck.

- You hope your children will have a positive impact on the people closest to them and the world.

You should have the same kind of hope for your business—that it is always in a position of strength and confidence based on sound financial footing with sufficient reserves to capitalize on opportunities and protect against unlikely, unwelcome events. A business needs to be protected, just as you watch over and protect your children. Likewise, sometimes it must be micromanaged while at other times it needs a longer leash. Just as a person hopes to build wealth, strength, and confidence, a business should build the same.

We call this process "building wealth" because, for most of us, our business wealth needs to be built one brick or one layer at a time. Wealth and strength rarely come in unexpected windfalls and nearly always are the result of discipline, sacrifice, hard work, and planning. If your goal is to have $100,000 in a bank or retirement account, you can't spend all of your money every month. You need to build that savings in $100, $1,000, or $10,000 increments over time.

Planning For Downturns

Protecting against the downside is important and too often overlooked. Statistically, recessions hit about every 10 years. Some are worse than others, of course, but they do occur with predictable frequency. Planning your company's approach if the financial situation deteriorates doesn't have to be an emotional acknowledgment that a downside is coming. Instead, think of it as good, thorough planning.

I've worked with business owners who didn't want to give any attention to the risk that their company's position could deteriorate. Doing so, they reasoned, would detract from the 100 percent optimism and focus necessary to keep the business going strong. I think that's stupid. When that kind of mindset gets confronted by an unexpected challenge—such as a key customer failing to pay his or her bills or   a lawsuit against the business or an overall downturn affecting your industry—the stage is set for an otherwise good business to close its doors.

A savvy business owner sets his or her business up to maximize success when something positive happens and to minimize failure if something bad occurs. It's that simple. Failing to do so is what I call the "ostrich theory," which is based on the well-known (but false) adage that an ostrich will bury its head in the sand to avoid danger, pretending no real problem exists. By comparison, in my experience, the most successful business owners are those who promote the approach of candor, transparency, and preparation.

Sadly, good businesses that are loved by customers, that have great missions, and that are staffed by passionate employees close their doors all the time. The ability to keep any business running is a simple math equation, one that must factor cash inflows minus cash outflows in relation to all of the cash an owner can come up with to loan the business when the company's bank account hits zero.

If there is a deep level of additional capital to contribute to the company, such a business might be able to survive while losing money for a long time. Of course, even when an owner has an incredibly strong desire to put a struggling company on his or her shoulders to carry it back to success, at the point a company runs out of cash and the next payroll is $100,000, there just may not be enough money left in the owner's personal bank account to turn the corner back to profitability.

When I started a small business earlier in my career, my rule was to put three percent of gross margin into savings each month. Early on, the amount was fairly insignificant. After a year, though, I'd built up a little reserve. After two years, I had the flexibility to make some decisions that favored the long-term success of the company at the cost of a little cash commitment up front.

Building such a cash reserve for your business is one of the ways to protect against downturns.

There's a difference between being a profitable business and having the cash to operate. If I run a business that consistently earns $50,000/month in revenue with expenses of $40,000/month, I have a profitable business. However, if I borrow $100,000 to cover my cash needs while my top customer doesn't pay its bills for a few months, my business is at risk if that customer ultimately goes bankrupt and doesn't pay me what is owed. In that scenario, I'm the one stuck with $100,000 in debt, monthly principal and interest payments, and a significant loss in anticipated revenue. Now my business is only one small mishap away from not having the cash to make its next payroll or to pay a key supplier before that supplier cuts off delivery.

When a company can't fund its payroll or a key supplier, the demise of that company can come quickly once employees stop coming to work or the supplies needed to fulfill the next job don't arrive.

As is true with many of the discussions in this book, not all suggestions and rules apply to all businesses. Some businesses find a unique niche, such as a technology or software company. Their approach might be to borrow significant amounts of money to grow exponentially and sell the company for an enormous price in just a few years. Other businesses are never intended to become an entity that can outlive its owner, and the sole purpose of the business is to deliver all the profits in the company to the owner each quarter, leaving no excess in the company. A small business that is financially backed by a billionaire or wealthy investors may not need to protect against any downside risk because there are infinitely deep pockets to provide that kind of support. (I once saw on a company's Balance Sheet that they had spent $100 million with no revenue. They were funded by investors to develop technology and build something innovative. A couple of years later, they sold that technology to a public company for $400 million.)

For most business owners, once the business gets beyond the initial challenges of its founding and has developed a recipe to bring in customers and become profitable, one of the strategic areas of focus should always be on making sure the business will still be viable in 10, 20, or 30 years. The closer any business moves from Level 2 to Level 4, the more that long-term focus needs to be an integral part of the strategic decision making.

When consideration of the long game of keeping the business alive indefinitely is regularly part of a company's strategic approach, the decisions its managers make are likely to differ from those made when the focus is on the short term. Business owners who are mindful of the steps necessary to make sure their companies are still around in the decades to come are more likely to succeed in their endeavors than those who aren't.

To some, this long-term, defensive approach might sound like the conservative rant of a CFO type rather than the aggressive attitude that comes more naturally to a sales-oriented CEO who wants to take over the world. I beg to differ. Consider the words of Bo Burlingham in his book Small Giants: Companies That Choose To Be Great Instead Of Big: "We all need a little accountant inside of us, saying, 'Hey, asshole, what are you doing?'"

You already know that half of all businesses don't make it past five years. The whole point of encouraging business owners to plan for the long game is to provide them with encouragement and wisdom so they can thrive rather than become just another statistic of failure. Do you think the businesses that fail within five years are the conservative ones that actively plan to protect themselves from downside risks, or the aggressive go-getters who think adding 15 percent to revenue this year is more important than building a firm foundation?

135

Cash Flow And Profit Strategy

The first and most important rule of business financial management is that you can only spend on expenses and cash outflows the money that comes in as revenue, unless you're making up the difference through loans or other types of investments. Thus, over time, if your cash out exceeds your cash in, you will either run out of money, go deeper into debt, or need to sell some of the ownership stake in your business.

In this way, business financial management is just like personal financial management. If you're regularly spending more than you bring in, you're in trouble and need to act before you run out of cash and find that you still haven't solved the problem.

When you're tracking your revenue and expenses and your cash inflows and outflows, there will be a lot of times that the summarized results tell you just what you were expecting. That's great. Don't take that as a sign that the bookkeeping doesn't need to be done or the cash flow doesn't need to be tracked. Over time, it is important for business managers to understand the size of the gap between inflows and outflows, revenues, and expenses. This balance must be positive (inflows exceeding outflows) or alternatively must be where the business manager deliberately wants the balance to be based on the intentional strategy of the company. If the balance is not where it should be, the company needs to increase revenues sufficiently to pay for the level of expense or the business must cut expenses to match the level of inflows (or do a little of both).

Word to the wise: I'm using the terms "revenues" and "expenses" a bit interchangeably with "cash inflows" and "outflows." They are similar but not the same.

Revenue is the income a business has earned from providing a good or service to a customer. If I provide a housecleaning service and I clean your house according to the quality level we have agreed upon, I earn revenue by completing my service. I still need to collect the cash.

- Some businesses collect cash at the time they earn the revenue by nature, such as a retail store or online merchant that takes your credit card number at time of checkout.

- Some businesses allow a period of time between earning that revenue and collecting cash from the customer, which creates a timing difference and creates some risk for the business that it will not collect all of the cash in all situations.

The general assumption is that good businesses eventually collect all of the revenue they are owed in cash, thus my interchanging of those terms here on occasion.

Similarly, over time, a good company presumably will pay all of its expenses in cash. Of course, if a company's revenue doesn't exceed its expenses, the result is usually problematic (except for those rare situations where such an imbalance is deliberate).

However, even companies that do have revenue exceeding expenses still need to manage their cash inflows to exceed their cash outflows, because revenues that aren't collected in cash really don't count when it comes to having the cash to keep the business alive. In other words, saying that cash inflows need to exceed cash outflows is more accurate and perhaps more appropriate.

There are also ways businesses might spend that don't appear as expenses on their Income Statements, so it can be a bit misleading if the business owner is only watching revenue and expenses.

For example:

- Some company owners pay themselves (a cash outflow) using "owner distributions" or "distributions of profit," which are reductions in equity on the company's Balance Sheet rather than expenses on the Income Statement.

- Some companies might purchase significant pieces of equipment (cash outflows) that are recorded as assets (something a company owns) on their Balance Sheet rather than as expenses.

- When a company has loan repayments, those are reported as a reduction in liabilities (something the company owes) rather than as an expense.

Most importantly, cash is king. Businesses need it to operate. Companies that report revenue exceeding expenses can still run out of cash if all of the profits earned (and more) are being sent to the owner in the form of distributions, are being used to purchase assets, or are used to repay loans.

Cash Flow Positive Is The Goal

The ideal cash flow strategy for all businesses is to develop a recipe for becoming cash flow positive as much as possible—or, at a minimum, cash flow neutral. Cash flow neutral is when the cash outflows of a company are timed to match the cash inflows.

In many businesses, when negotiating with customers about whether the customer needs to provide an upfront deposit before starting a project, or the timing of when the customer would need

138

to make milestone payments, the negotiating position I suggest businesses take is they need to make the situation cash flow neutral to their company. That's a very reasonable negotiating position for most situations, and should be one of the anchoring principles on which a company is built. Without a recipe for revenue generation to at least be cash flow neutral, a business will need increasingly more cash the larger it grows.

A common philosophy exists that a business's main objective is to maximize profit. That's not false. It's mostly true . . . with some disclaimers.

In the eyes of the law, a company is an entity like a person. However, a business does not have emotions, desires, feelings, or thoughts. It is like a person, but it lacks many person-like characteristics. A large business that has investors (who expect maximum returns on their investments) doesn't get to feel good about donating to charity or feel less anxious when stockpiling cash in a rainy day fund. Those feelings are reserved for individuals in a company who may or may not have been given the authority by the board of directors to make those types of decisions. A business's job, at that level, is to maximize net income and return on investment to its shareholders. If donating profits to charity or stockpiling cash is the best strategy to maximize net income over the long term for the company, then that's a good decision. Otherwise, the company shouldn't do it because it doesn't maximize net income.

Smaller businesses, though, have a much grayer line between the owner/founder of the business and the business itself, such that the objective may not always be to maximize profit.

Imagine you're in your 20s and you move to Southern California for the great weather. Since you like to be outside, you decide you want to start making an income by cleaning pools. You knock on doors and sign up some nearby residents to pay you monthly for your service. Whenever you're not cleaning pools, you're hustling to add new business. Soon your schedule is full and you're making a nice income. Over the next couple of years, your customers keep telling their friends about your great service, so you hire some other pool cleaners and keep a margin for the work they do while the business and the revenue grows. Your overhead is minimal, so you get to keep most of the money the company brings in, other than what it pays your employees and the direct costs associated with servicing each pool.

As the company grows, you build a cash reserve to protect the business and your personal finances in case of a significant change—such as a whole group of clients in the same neighborhood deciding to leave you for a competitor all at once, or an opportunity to take on a series of apartment complexes at profitable prices if you offer them 60-day payment terms (which would require you to cover payroll for your pool cleaners before you collect from these customers, which would in turn necessitate having greater cash reserves on hand).

Now that you've saved a comfortable cash reserve, does your company need to continue to maximize net income?

As a general business principle, maximizing net income is a good idea for any company. For some companies, though, decisions can be made according to the values of the owner or the board of directors, which might be contrary to doing every last thing to maximize net income. The happiness of the owner/board now enters the decision- making mix, as do tax implications and other scenarios.

For example, what if a single-owner business earns $500,000 in net income in a year and the firm's tax expert says there will be significant reductions in current year taxes if the owner buys a Range Rover through the business before year's end. Does that make it OK to buy one? Sometimes it does, and sometimes it doesn't. The answer depends on the balance of many different measures of the financial health of both the owner and the business.

Other examples:

- The owner might want to buy a commercial building for the company, even though the expense would be more than the company would otherwise pay in rent. Why would he or she want to do this? Because doing so aligns with the owner's wealth building strategy.

- The owner might decide to donate a portion of proceeds to charity on behalf of the company, knowing that the company won't maximize net income compared to if it didn't make the donation.

- The owner might give himself a bonus each quarter, effectively taking profit out of the entity to transfer to his or her personal bank account.

As a good business principle, it is important to note that a business is not a charity (unless, of course, it is actually a nonprofit entity). Even for small businesses, any decision that does not maximize net income should be a deliberate one—and a lot of novice business owners get into trouble over this.

- If a company has a downturn and is overpaying by $10,000/ month for employees the company can live without, should it keep them anyway? For how long?

- If a company can change suppliers to save money, is there a good reason why the company shouldn't do so?

- If a company is paying for unnecessary costs, is there a good reason to keep paying them?

- If a company hasn't raised prices in two years, should it?

Maximizing net income as a small company is about being proactive enough to control the finances of your business instead of letting them control you. If you own a small business and you haven't raised prices in three years because you're afraid to lose the customers you love even though your costs increase each year, you may not be maximizing net income.

Whether in business or personal situations, it is much harder to save $100 than it is to spend $100, just like for most of us it's so much easier to gain weight than it is to lose.

The savvy, diligent business owner regularly asks and answers the question, "If our entire goal were just to maximize profit, what would we do differently?" In the perspective of experienced CEOs, all decisions are all about "the money" all of the time.

Every business owner at least needs to consider this perspective. That way, when business owners make exceptions that put their happiness ahead of profits in their single-owner businesses, they can recognize such exceptions as inherent to being the only owner of a small business vs. being the CEO of a public company.

Pricing

Charging the optimal price is among the most important decisions in running a business. It is a decision that needs to be reconsidered and revisited regularly. An increase in price of only a few percent can lead to a substantial percentage increase in net income. Prices impact profit margins and sales volume.

One pricing strategy to consider involves the balance between price vs. the likelihood of profitable execution of the work required for a customer. The more financially risky fulfillment is, the more margin the company should make if it executes properly.

To illustrate, let's use an example from the construction industry:

Imagine there are two construction companies. Each has been awarded a project.

In our first example, Company A is purchasing and installing a piece of equipment for a customer in which the cost of the equipment is the vast majority of the overall project cost. Company A has already locked in the price of the equipment, so it is known, confirmed, and will not change. Company A has also already confirmed a quoted cost from a subcontractor to install the equipment in which the subcontractor has agreed to accept all of the risk in the off chance the installation cost exceeds the quoted amount. Should it do so, the subcontractor has agreed to absorb all cost overruns and will not seek additional payment from the construction company.

In our second example, Company B has been asked to custom-build something for the client. Company B will do this from scratch, using its own direct labor hours, and a design that is new to them.

Both Company A and Company B have prepared budgets detailing the expected costs to complete each project. Which company should add a higher markup above its costs when preparing a quote for the customer?

For Company A, the risk that the job will lose money is very close to zero. Company A is essentially just passing through costs that are already fixed, so even if Company A quoted only $1 higher than the quotes received from its suppliers and subcontractors, Company A is virtually guaranteed to make $1.

For Company B, there's a much wider bell curve of possible outcomes. The project could wind up being much more profitable than planned, or it could result in losing money.

Putting aside for a moment that, in general, both companies should factor into their quotes the highest price point their customers would be willing to pay, Company B should quote its job at a much larger margin because there is greater risk that the job may or may not be completed as profitably as planned. On the other hand, Company A could quote a much lower margin.

Most construction companies quote and execute projects that are a combination of materials, labor, and subcontractors. As a general rule with construction companies, labor is always where the greatest risk of going over budget resides. The cost of materials (especially   if prices are locked in with suppliers at the inception of a job) and costs associated with subcontractors (if fixed price quotes are received) tend to be at lower risk of causing a project's costs to go overbudget. Therefore, when quoting construction jobs to customers, construction companies typically factor in a significant markup on labor and a much smaller markup on materials and subcontractors.

If I were running a construction company and I needed to decide on the prices to quote a customer for two jobs, each of which I expected to cost me $750,000 to fulfill, I might quote a job that is 80 percent materials and 20 percent labor at $900,000 while for a job that is 20 percent materials and 80 percent labor, I might quote it closer to $1.1 million. The reason for the difference is simple: the risk that the job with 80 percent labor won't be as profitable as planned is much higher than the risk with the job involving only 20 percent labor.

This yin and yang of risk and pricing applies across other industries and business models. For example, I've worked with businesses that provide custom software programming services to other large businesses. In those situations, I've often told customers, "The lowest price I can possibly give you is one in which we charge you for each hour rather than a fixed price, because that assures us you're going to pay for every single hour our team works. If you'd like us to take some risk that the job will be done at a certain price, by definition we need to increase our margin at least a little bit to cover the additional risk that we're taking."

Raising Prices Over Time

In addition to knowing how to calculate prices, businesses also need to consider raising their prices every year (a scenario often not considered by business owners). In fact, most businesses should be raising prices by at least two percent every year. After all, costs generally go up for businesses by this amount (or more) annually—plus the prices for groceries, utilities, and consumer products go up as well. Why should your company's prices stay flat?

Many business owners and managers fear that raising prices will lead to adverse consequences. In some environments, that is possible and needs to be considered. In my experience, though, business owners place way too much weight on the fear that adverse consequences will come to their businesses as a result of raising prices and not nearly enough weight on the positive impact raising prices will have.

Let's look at a couple of examples to explain the impact of raising prices on the financial health of a business.

As a base case starting point, assume a business earns the following:

Revenue	$100,000
Cost of Goods Sold	$60,000
Gross Profit	$40,000
Gross Profit Margin	40%
SG&A Expenses	$25,000
Net Income	$15,000

Now, assume the business raises prices by five percent and has no customer loss. Now the business earns:

Revenue (5% higher than the base case)	$105,000
Cost of Goods Sold (no change in cost)	$60,000
Gross Profit	$45,000
Gross Profit Margin	43%
SG&A Expenses (no change in cost)	$25,000
Net Income	$20,000

Yes, you are reading correctly: by raising prices five percent, the company increased its net income by 25 percent!

Let's now figure how much volume of revenue the company can

lose at these higher prices before it is making the same level of Net Income that existed before the price increase?

The answer is 11 percent of the customer volume would need to leave after the price increase for the company to earn the same Net Income. Let's prove it with math:

Revenue (11% reduction from $105k)	$93,000
Cost of Goods Sold (now at a 43% margin)	$53,000
Gross Profit	$40,000
Gross Profit Margin (new margin level)	43%
SG&A Expenses (no change in cost)	$25,000
Net Income	$15,000

As you can see, pricing is important. The numbers clearly demonstrate that even a small price increase that comes with a small loss in customer volume is more profitable for a business than no price increase at all.

Price Increase Example

	(A) Base	(B) 5% ↑ No Cost Loss	(C) 5% ↑ 11% Cost Loss
Revenue	100,000	105,000	93,333
COGS	60,000	60,000	53,333
Margin $	**40,000**	**45,000**	**40,000**
Margin %	40%	43%	43%
SG&A Expense	25,000	25,000	25,000
Net Operating Income	**15,000**	**20,000**	**15,000**
Other Income/Expenses	0	0	0
Net Income	**15,000**	**20,000**	**15,000**

Conclusion:

Scenario B increases prices by 5%, but increases net income by 25% over the Base Scenario A. Scenario C can see a 11% decrease in volume vs Scenario B to still reach the net income of Scenario A.

Markup vs. Margin

Understanding the difference between Margin and Markup is mission critical for many business owners, and it can be confusing. This guidance will try to make it simple.

The critical distinction between Margin and Markup is as follows:

- Margin is a mathematical function of revenue.

- Markup is a mathematical function of cost.

By definition, they cannot be the same. They must be different.

Important: At the end of the day, what you care about is Margin. Keep that in mind as we explore how they both work.

Margin

When you read an Income Statement for your business, you'll see or calculate:

- Revenue

- Cost of Goods Sold

- Gross Profit

- Gross Profit Margin

So, the income statement might say:

Revenue	$25,000
Cost of Goods Sold	$15,000
Gross Profit ($25k minus $15k)	$10,000
Gross Profit Margin	40%

Next, you'd typically decide whether 40 percent is good or bad for your company (which we won't get into here). The key to this exercise is the Gross Profit Margin—or Margin—which is 40 percent of revenue, calculated as $10,000 in Gross Profit divided by $25,000 in Revenue.

Markup

When you're establishing the price to charge a customer, you're usually working with Markup. Markup works as follows:

- My cost to do this job/project (COGS) is $4,000.

- I'll mark up my cost by 40 percent ($4,000 x 40 percent = $1,600 Markup).

- Therefore, my sales price to the customer is $5,600 ($4,000 cost + $1,600 Markup).

The critical distinction to know is this: when you mark up your cost 40 percent, that won't give you a margin of 40 percent, that will give you a margin of 28.6 percent. Yikes!

If this is the only job you do in a particular month, the income statement would look like this:

Revenue (the sales price to the customer)	$5,600
Cost of Goods Sold	$4,000
Gross Profit (in dollars, that equals the markup)	$1,600
Gross Profit Margin ($1,600/$5,600)	28.6%

To get a 40 percent Margin, you need the sales price to be $6,667. This provides a Gross Margin (aka gross profit) of $2,667 which, when divided by $6,667 (sales price), equals 40 percent. That means your Markup needs to be 67 percent, not 40 percent.

How The Calculation Works

To turn cost into Margin, the equation to do on your calculator is:

- Cost / (1-desired Margin) = sales price to the customer
  Using our example:

- $4,000 in cost / (1 – 40% desired Margin) = $6,667

On our website, www.TheNumbersEdge.com, we have a "Margin vs. Markup" converter in Excel format available in the downloads area.

Other Fundamental Tactics

If running a business with ever-increasing financial health were as easy as a snap of the fingers, everyone would be doing it and 50 percent of companies wouldn't go out of business within five years. Success depends on much more than good bookkeeping and analyzing results. Getting the entire recipe right is quite challenging and often takes years to refine—that's even if the owner's version of success is actually ever achieved.

No single recipe, trick, or tactic that might enhance success for one business necessarily applies to all others. There are thousands of books written to guide business owners towards improving their sales, marketing, business management, cost efficiency, and overall business "secret sauce."

From the 30,000-foot view, all businesses should, and eventually will, develop formulas of operation that are unique to them even if unwritten or not clearly defined. From a financial perspective, the key is to get that formula to churn out results that meet the goals of the owner(s).

Here are some additional concepts that may help:

What Revenue Is Good Revenue?

The first and most obvious rule that all businesses should follow is keep your revenue up and your expenses down. If you don't keep your expenses lower than your revenue, you're bound for major problems and stress. It's much easier to spend a dollar than it is to save a dollar. Business owners should be shrewd and tight when it comes to spending money, and should be assertive and opportunistic to bring money in.

Most businesses do not enhance their success over the long term by accepting all revenue and by "being all things to all people." Granted, when businesses are in their infant stages, they may gravitate towards saying "yes" to any and all customers and client requests (even when not ideal), but over time a business typically increases success when it specializes in one or a few certain niches or market segments. This allows for development of a high technical ability to serve a specific sector, and can enhance marketing efforts by demonstrating a specialty area of focus. In plain English, you need to know what your business is really good at. If you have trouble answering that concisely, refining that answer should be part of your near-term goals. You can't please everybody. If that's what you're chasing, you'll fail. Focus on customers who like you . . . and on work that you like doing.

It's also not unusual for there to be a disconnect between what a business owner thinks everyone should love and what customers actually show they love by how they spend their dollars. That's why businesses need to change and adapt over time. In fact, most businesses will need to do this in order to maximize success or even survive. Some will even get into totally different businesses from where they began.

As your business grows and evolves, you'll need to test what customers seek, desire, and are willing to pay for. This is one of the reasons restaurants change their menus occasionally and businesses try new product offerings. The marketing term for it is A/B testing, which refers to comparing the same process with one of the variables changed in Situation A vs. Situation B to see which is more successful. All companies should be mindful of A/B testing opportunities. They should consider new product offerings, new ways to make money, and new segments of their potential customer base to target—but they should not fall into the trap of saying "yes" every time a customer asks for something unique.

Part of the reason and need for slicing and dicing financial analysis by product, job, or other variables is to determine how to balance demand with pricing. If a store sells 50 different jewelry pieces, shouldn't it know what the revenue and margin is for each one? Shouldn't it look for the common attributes of its most popular pieces to fill the store with products customers love?

Undoubtedly, a business shouldn't sell a product to a customer where the sales price is less than the cost. A mentor of mine calls this "Selling a $20 bill for $18." In some respects, this is obvious. Who would deliberately sell a $20 bill for $18? In some businesses, if the accounting isn't accurate, this mistake can be made more easily because the cost of the $20 bill isn't as clear as reading the amount on the face of it.

For example, on Season 1, Episode 2 of *The Profit*, Marcus Lemonis discussed the cost and pricing at a flower shop:

- The cost of putting together a particular arrangement used to be $75. It was sold for $85.

- Over time, the costs for the individual materials and labor increased, but the price to the customer did not.

- Eventually, the florist was selling the arrangement at no profit and didn't even realize it.

Word to the wise: when the direct materials and labor to create a product sum to $85 and the sales price for that product is less than $85, that's essentially the same as "selling a $20 bill for $18."

Revenue Filters

One of the CFOs I've learned from likes to use an analogy where he likens the filter for your pool to the filter a business should have for its revenue. The pool filter is not an optional component of the pool system. It is in every single pool system, just as all companies should have some kind of revenue filter. The pool filter keeps out unwanted influences, so the water stays clean and desirable. Such is the intention of a revenue filter.

Here are some examples of revenue filters a business can use:

- Incentive systems that favor desired customer attributes for salespeople or operations team members, such as higher sales commissions on new clients that produce a Gross Margin above 55 percent, or bonuses for jobs completed by spending less than the estimated budget for the job

- Having individuals or processes be accountable to accept only desired customers and revenue at the company, such as a quarterly executive customer list review meeting

- Monitoring the profitability of customers.

One of the important revenue filters all businesses should have is to accept only customers who will pay what they owe. Of course, if we knew which customers weren't going to pay their bills, we would never take them on as customers in the first place, so it isn't quite as easy as it sounds. Dealing with accounts receivable, collections, and delinquent customers can be time consuming, frustrating, and expensive. It should be minimized.

Here are some ways to minimize the risk of providing a service or product to customers who won't pay, and to minimize the administrative time and cost associated with collections activities:

- Develop a credit verification procedure that analyzes, grades, and decides whether each new customer is credit worthy.

- Control customer payments by getting pre-authorizations to charge their bank accounts via ACH or a credit card on file. The downside of charging a credit card on file is the merchant processing fees, which essentially reduce Gross Profit Margin by three to four percent. When possible, charge customers a credit card surcharge for paying by card (some states permit a credit card surcharge to be charged; others do not). ACH has very low fees compared to charging credit cards, but may have setup requirements, amount limits, and may be resisted by some customers who are hesitant to allow vendors to charge their bank accounts directly. Having a revenue filter involves making decisions such as whether the business should accept customers who won't allow their bank accounts or credit cards to be charged automatically according to the agreed-upon payment terms.

- Charge late fees when payments are not received on time.

- Stay on top of customers who haven't paid by their due dates. Communicate proactively when those payment due dates are approaching. Communicate directly, outside of email, when a payment has not arrived by the due date. Communicate frequently after the due date passes.

- Shut off future services or order processing promptly when prior bills are still outstanding past their due dates.

- Review Accounts Receivable reports weekly. Process payments from customers in the accounting system daily so that Accounts Receivable reports are accurate. Designate a person in the company to be in charge of keeping Accounts Receivable reports updated, following up with late paying customers, and communicating key concerns from that report to the business owner weekly.

- Require down payment or full payment at the time of the order or transaction. A customer who doesn't want to leave any down payment at time of order may be at higher risk not to pay at all. At least a customer who provides a down payment shows initial good faith in his or her intention to pay.

The Cost Of Collecting

For many businesses, it is more profitable to sell to customers on credit than not to sell at all. Similarly, the cost of collections plus bad debt write-offs for customers who don't pay can be lower overall than the incremental Gross Margin earned because the business offers payment terms.

However, spending inordinate amounts of time on collections and Accounts Receivable detracts from the simplicity of running a business, and a business manager should strive to maintain simplicity in operating procedures whenever possible. Collections challenges add to overhead, increase the Breakeven Point, and may use the time of the business owner or senior managers that could be better spent on more profitable initiatives.

Watch Your Overhead

A larger company, with more revenue, is not necessarily a better company than a smaller one. I'd rather own a company that has $50 million a year in sales and $20 million in net income than a company that has $100 million in sales and $5 million in net income any day of the week—unless someone can show me that the second company is going to have more net income in future years than the first one, or has a larger market value that coincides with the owner's intentions to sell the business.

Businesses with lower overhead are far less stressful for owners and less risky compared to businesses that require higher levels of revenue to stay above their breakeven points. Overhead costs that stay fixed and level through both profitable times and downcycles can kill companies during downcycles. To the extent expenses can be highly flexible to revenue, that's strongly preferable. That keeps the Breakeven Point as low as possible, which is ideal.

For example, it's generally better to pay as many staff as possible a lower base plus variable compensation that fluctuates with the performance of the company so that expenses naturally rise when revenue is up and expenses naturally lower when revenue is down.

The best business models are generally structured such that whichever party has the higher risk in a situation gets to keep more of the profit or margin.

For example, if I hire a salesperson who insists on having a higher base, he or she isn't going to earn as high of a percentage of revenue as a commission compared to someone who has no base and earns a commission only. The commission-only salesperson takes all of the risk, so if he or she performs well, that person should be able to make more money. The salesperson who wants a higher base is putting the company more at risk because, in a down month, the company still needs to pay him or her a certain base amount. In such a scenario, the salesperson with a base salary might make an additional three percent of sales while the commission-only salesperson might make five percent of sales as his or her commission.

Principles

Decisions to be made when presented with tricky situations about whether to make exceptions for a potential customer's request for unusual payment terms, or on how to handle an ethical issue, or to what type of revenue the business should say "no," are helped if the leader or leaders of a business have already thought through the company's principles in advance.

Examples of principles that I have seen guide the decisions of business owners and their businesses include the following:

- We will not take customers who do not provide down payments up front. A down payment shows a customer's willingness to work with us and pay us for the work we will perform.

- We will not take customers who don't agree that we can draw payments from their bank accounts according to our standard payment terms. Creating exceptions to this adds risk to our standard operating procedures and increases overhead. That's not the way we want to do business.

- We will not work with people who lie to us or steal from us, even if it is a small amount. Making small exceptions leads us down a slippery slope.

- I will take two vacations a year with my family. The constant pressure from the needs of business will not compromise this commitment.

- We will maintain bookkeeping and financial standards that inform management about the financial health of the business. These are the navigation tools we need to steer the ship.

- We won't be a business that gives raises only when someone tells us he or she is quitting. We will proactively pay our team members fair wages, and we will benchmark wages annually to know what is fair compared to peers, whether employees ask for pay increases or not.

Whether you're running a business, being an employee, or managing your family or personal life, each day you make decisions that you think are the right step in the right direction. After a couple of years, you might look back at the path you have walked and wonder, "How did I end up here? This isn't where I intended to be!"

Establishing principles at the beginning of your journey is akin to drawing a map to show the way forward. Having these guiding principles in place and adhering to them provides a reference in case following your compass each day proves difficult or seems to be steering you a little bit off course.

When you have ideas in mind about the future you'd like for your business, your employees, and yourself, or when you have principles and a framework to guide decisions when the right answer is unclear, I encourage you to share those with your team. Don't assume the people around you know what is in your head. This is why companies choose to write mission statements, vision statements, and guiding principles. The goal is to get everyone headed in the same direction you are headed (vision), for the same reasons you are going there (mission), using the same recipe (principles).

Principles and direction can always be changed. You can start a business deciding you'll take certain types of customers or offer certain types of products, and adapt when that doesn't go as planned. But the goals, boundaries, and ethics of a company typically stay fairly constant over time. These principles will provide the best guidance if they are acknowledged in advance and referred to often to keep the company, and you, heading down the right path.

PULLING IT ALL TOGETHER

When a business has integrated the fundamentals of financial management into its rhythm, and when its operators know their KPIs and their numbers both historically and forecasted, opportunities arise that other companies which operate without this level of financial acumen never encounter.

- A company that manages by numbers is better positioned to add investors or borrow money because its management and ownership can communicate with knowledge and confidence about the positive financial reasons why others should want a stake in the business.

- The company's likelihood of running out of cash or going out of business is reduced because measures are taken to prevent the company from being in a position of undue risk.

- Profits improve because owners and managers understand and can identify the highly profitable areas of the business compared to the less profitable ones.

- The company has a clear financial roadmap, rooted in reasonable assumptions and candid considerations about the future.

A business with a clear recipe for attracting customers and providing products and/or services to them profitably typically wants to attract *more* customers as quickly as possible, or to apply more of its available cash towards customer acquisition rather than to use it as a safety net. A business at this stage might seek additional protection in the form of a loan or line of credit from a bank.

Word to the wise: a business that manages by numbers is much better positioned to get a loan than a business without a fundamental understanding of its own financials.

Getting A Loan

Banks are in the business of "not losing money" . . . ever. They only want to lend when they are 100 percent certain they are going to be repaid. When loaning money to a business, a bank will attempt to identify secondary or tertiary sources of repayment in case the business doesn't pay back the loan based on its operations, such as requiring a personal guarantee from the owner or adding a security interest to a property.

A bank's perspective is very logical. No lender ever wants to loan money to a business when there's a good chance of not getting the money back. Nor does a lender want to loan money to a business that is losing money just to help that business find more time to turn the business around.

Banks want to loan money to businesses that have demonstrated a history of profitability and available cash flow and who are using the available money to accelerate success. Banks are not in the business of speculation, hope, or investment. Banks have no problem saying "no" to opportunities that don't meet their criteria.

Banks also aren't really interested in taking possession of any backup collateral they secured as a method of recovering losses. For example, taking possession of a company's inventory and selling it to get the loan repaid is expensive, difficult, and risky. Banks prefer an easier route. They want to know they'll get a check each month from the borrower. That's why they prefer to do the hard work before they loan any money.

- If your company's need for cash is based on what you think, expect, plan, or hope will happen with no track record or demonstrated success, you should not expect a bank to lend to you.

- If your company's need for cash is demonstrated by a clear recipe for future profitability, matched with a Balance Sheet that shows the company owns much more than it owes, you have a good chance of securing a loan.

Banks are typically very willing to lend money when a company has a high amount of equity, especially when that equity is tied up in something other than cash, such as accounts receivable, inventory, or recently purchased equipment. From the bank's perspective, these situations mean a high probability of repayment.

When a company cannot demonstrate the kind of financial strength a bank requires for a loan, there are non-bank lenders that provide loans in riskier, more speculative situations. These loans require much higher interest rates because the risk to the lender is greater. Non- bank lending is typical for companies with a history of demonstrated success, but that might have made one or two mistakes along the way, resulting in a decline in equity on their Balance Sheet. If convinced such mistakes have been corrected, some non-bank lenders might be willing to take a chance.

If your company seeks a referral to lenders, feel free to email us at care@thenumbersedge.com and we'd be happy to refer you to the lenders we've worked with.

Deterring & Detecting Fraud

Fraud occurs at an alarmingly high percentage of businesses in the United States and the reason is simple: a business that does not track or understand its numbers is wide open to fraud.

According to the 2015/16 Global Fraud Report by Kroll Inc., a multi-national, corporate investigations and risk consulting firm, 75 percent of the 768 business owners surveyed reported fraud in their companies in the past year.

Fraud risks to small businesses are higher than the risk to larger companies. According to the Association of Certified Fraud Examiner's (ACFE) 2014 Report to the Nations on Occupational Fraud and Abuse, "Small businesses are both disproportionately victimized by fraud and notably under-protected by anti-fraud controls, a combination that makes them significantly vulnerable to this threat." ACFE's research indicates that more than 50 percent of small businesses have a primary weakness in either "Lack of Internal Controls" or "Lack of Management Review." ACFE reports that small businesses, defined as 100 employees or fewer, suffered a median loss of $154,000 per fraud loss. Small businesses are less likely to have hotlines, internal audit departments, external audits, and CFO level expertise reviewing the accounting and financial reporting monthly. Fraud is real, and everyone who gets victimized by it thinks, "I never thought it would happen to me!"

If you own a small business, what can you do to avoid becoming a fraud victim like the majority of your peers?

The cornerstone to deterring and detecting fraud is in your accounting—the hub through which all transactions flow and the area of the company that controls the cash. Here are some best practices in bookkeeping to deter and detect fraud.

Best Practice 1: Reconcile The Bank Accounts Every Day

Most bookkeepers reconcile the bank accounts monthly, when the bank sends the statement. The best practice is to look up the online balance every day, and actually reconcile to that in your accounting system. This way every transaction that hits the bank account is identified immediately. Reconciling the bank account should be the first task of the morning for your bookkeeper, done by 9:00 am, every day.

The most common objection to this is that reconciliations are traditionally done to bank statement balances, and the statements only come out once a month. Dismiss the traditional thinking and reconcile it daily. We live in an age of online banking.

One way that companies can be defrauded is when someone steals check stock and eventually forges a check. Out of a couple of hundred companies I've been involved with, I've only seen it happen twice in the past five years—but it does happen. The last time this occurred, because we were reconciling daily, we noticed the very next morning that a check had cleared our bank that we didn't have recorded in our accounting system. We were able to call the bank immediately. Without daily reconciliation procedures, this fraud might have been caught weeks later in the monthly reconciliation, when it would have been too late for the bank to resolve it in our favor—or perhaps it would have been glossed over as an anomaly in the month-end reconciliation process all together.

Best Practice 2: Match Checks To Source Documents Before You Sign Them

When signing checks, the vendor invoice or source document should be paper-clipped to it. The check signer should compare the vendor name, date, and dollar amount between the system-generated check and invoice before signing. If your company is large enough that other department managers can approve vendor invoices, evidence of that approval should also be attached to the check. If all of it isn't together, don't sign the check. Train your bookkeeper through your check signing practices that you only sign checks where *all* of the documentation is in order.

One common method of bookkeeping fraud is to make payments to fraudulent vendors, or to pay an incorrect amount to vendors in combination with another transaction that eventually puts money in the account of the person perpetrating the fraud. Requiring all documentation to be included with checks, and verifying the consistency of the numbers, is a great deterrent.

It should go without saying that the person printing checks should never also sign the checks. Also, the person who prints the checks should not be the same person who reconciles the bank account.

Best Practice 3: Require A Second Set Of Eyes

A second person who has a good understanding of accounting (Controller or CFO level) should thoroughly review the accounting transactions and records monthly. A bookkeeper working alone—especially one who is well-qualified—knows how to steal money if he or she were to choose to. Even if you have a deep personal trust for your bookkeeper, the prudent approach is to build a system such that no one person could steal if he or she became motivated to do so. Having an independent accounting expert thoroughly research both the inputs (transaction level) and the output (review of the financial statements) is a significant deterrent to any bookkeeper considering committing fraud. It isn't sufficient just to have a tax preparer who analyzes the output at the end of the process. All businesses need oversight from someone who is thoroughly trained in how to drill down to the transaction level when a questionable situation is identified, and has the motivation to trace an unusual finding all the way to the source document.

If you'd like an interesting example of this, search for "Leucadia Pizzeria fraud" on Google. The bookkeeper hired by Leucadia Pizzeria didn't have any oversight. After stealing $450,000, she got caught when she fell ill and another bookkeeper needed to take over to keep the accounting on schedule. Interestingly, that perpetrator actually applied to and was hired at a company where my colleagues were running the accounting. That business had sufficient CFO level oversight, though, which must have been clear once she got there. After two days on the job, she never came back. We never knew why she stopped coming to work until we saw her name in the newspaper years later, from the Leucadia Pizzeria incident.

Best Practice 4: The Balance Sheet Needs To Be Reconciled Monthly

For most business owners, the Balance Sheet is something between a black hole no one understands and a nuisance that only technical accountants care about. At most companies, it's incredibly easy for money to get lost in all the numbers, totals, and sub-totals, and even when balance anomalies are brought up—especially if they are relatively small—they are typically just written off to expense.

The best practice is for the bookkeeper to identify exactly what makes up the balance in every single Balance Sheet account every month—no ambiguities, no ignored accounts. Every dollar should be accounted for precisely on a spreadsheet for every account.

At best, 10 percent of small businesses do this. That's part of the reason why some 75 percent of small businesses (per the 2015/16 Kroll report) experience fraud. Don't assume that just because other small businesses neglect the discipline of Balance Sheet reconciliation, it's OK for yours to do it too.

Best Practice 5: Require Tight Credit Card Controls

Best practices around credit cards have many significant benefits to the business owner but are rarely implemented, especially in small businesses. Fraud perpetrated through credit card use is less about deliberate, blatant stealing, and more about the leakage of cash through the gray areas of using the company card for non-business transactions.

In the context of credit card transactions that originate from a cardholder other than the business owner, the IRS and business owners actually agree that credit card transactions should only be ordinary and necessary in the course of operating the business, and that receipts, documentation, and explanations are needed to explain why a transaction is ordinary and necessary for the business. Therefore, tight credit card controls should involve standard operating procedures that assure the credit card is used only for necessary business purposes.

Additionally, the documentation that every transaction is ordinary and necessary for the business will prevent the IRS from disallowing transactions previously reported as business expenses on the tax return in the event of an audit.

In specific:

- Receipts should always be collected. Every receipt should have a hand-written note about the specific business purpose for the transaction (the more explanation, the better). Your bookkeeper should track which transactions have a receipt and which don't, and should be able to produce a list of transactions without receipts in a moment's notice.

- Don't share cards. Whoever might use a card should have a card issued in his or her name to maximize accountability in tracking transactions. If you don't want the person to actually carry the card, keep it under lock and key and give it out only for specifically approved transactions.

- Your bookkeeper should review all credit card transactions daily or weekly, not monthly.

- Each transaction should be input into your accounting system individually, not as a batch entry at the end of the month— especially if you use an accounting system that can download the transactions automatically, such as QuickBooks.

- A list of all credit card transactions should be sent to the CEO monthly or more often for review.

The implications of loose credit card controls are significant. When the IRS performs an audit, one of the first places they look is for undocumented meal transactions. Those transactions can be retroactively disallowed as tax deductible business expenses, with fines and penalties added on top. A multi-year audit can leave a business owner holding a five-figure bill from the IRS based on the bad credit card practices of employees who aren't even with the company any longer!

When credit card users feel that the controls over credit card expenses are loose, the risk factor for use of the card on questionable transactions increases. If a cardholder knows no one is looking at the transactions each month, do you think he or she will be more or less inclined to run a personal charge through the card occasionally?

The real best practice in business is don't use company credit cards at all. Require employees to use their own credit cards to front the cost for discretionary expenses and have a policy of promptly providing reimbursement when an expense report is submitted and approved.

Top Methods Of Bookkeeper Fraud

Fraud can get quite elaborate, but most fraud can be deterred and detected with some basic, time-tested practices. Knowing how fraud commonly occurs drives the strategy for how to prevent it. Any good bookkeeper knows how to commit fraud, and in environments where the likelihood of getting caught is high, by necessity the fraud will be more complex and the person's motivation to steal quite high.

Knowing how bookkeepers might steal can help deter it from happening in the first place. Here are some of the top ways bookkeepers steal from businesses:

- **Printing checks to fictitious vendors.** In this scenario, a check is signed by an authorized individual, but it is paid unwittingly to a "fake" vendor. Usually the fictitious vendor is for a company (or companies) created by the bookkeeper. Dollar amounts are typically low enough so that someone reading the income statement doesn't notice. If the bookkeeper does this well, there's a fairly small charge paid to the fake vendor routinely, creating consistency. It isn't unusual for fictitious invoices to be created. It is also possible at some companies for a bookkeeper to pay a fictitious vendor by forging a signature, using a signature stamp, or perhaps even having signing authority him- or herself. If someone does forge a check or release an unauthorized payment, it's going to show up on the bank statement. So always require that the person who reconciles the bank account be someone other than the person who prints the checks. Also, someone else should open the bank statements when they arrive and look for unusual transactions.

- **Charging unauthorized expenses on a company credit card.** Even if your bookkeeper doesn't have a company credit card, he or she probably has access to a company credit card number. Most commonly in terms of fraud, credit cards are used to purchase personal items such as personal meals, gas for personal vehicles, and inexpensive personal items. If that goes unnoticed, the next level is to use the card to pay to take the family out for a nice dinner or to buy more expensive items or gift cards. When a credit card statement arrives, the business owner or a qualified manager should review the statement. If anything looks unusual, investigate. There should be a different card for every person who might use one, even if you keep them all under lock and key. This increases accountability and reduces time to figure out which transactions were charged by which employees. Set the tone in your company that receipts are required for every credit card transaction.

- **Paying unauthorized amounts through payroll.** In many small businesses, the bookkeeper runs payroll and approves payroll. Any employee can fill out an overstated time sheet, including a bookkeeper—and a bookkeeper can pay a friend more than that friend's timecard says by modifying the hours, rate, or overtime. To control this, payroll for all employees should be approved by the managers of those employees, including the bookkeeper's time. It should be the standard practice that someone else reviews every payroll report. Knowing that someone else is paying attention to the payroll report is a significant deterrent to committing payroll fraud. Another common method of fraud is failing to record vacation time used, which overstates the employee's vacation balance, and overstates the payout the employee receives when he or she leaves.

- **Stealing cash.** Most cash is stolen in businesses that deal with a lot of cash, such as retail stores or businesses with cash registers, or in businesses that have petty cash. These days, petty cash has been eliminated at most well-run businesses. I strongly suggest doing away with it. Employees can fill out expense reports and get reimbursed rather than asking for cash from a petty cash drawer. If you do have petty cash, have a person who oversees accounting sign off on the reconciliation of it monthly, checking for receipts and documentation for every purchase. When you have a cash register, it may not be the bookkeeper who steals, but there's still ample opportunity for undetected theft. If you have a business with a cash register and you can change to credit card only transactions, that's ideal. If you do accept cash, put a security camera over your cash registers to deter and detect theft. Require management approval for all credits or voids.

Hiring A CFO

When your business is of the appropriate size to hire a Chief Financial Officer, everything you've read here will be part of the institutional knowledge and standard routine for that individual. This is the playbook for what CFOs already know well—and this is just the easy part of the playbook.

Most organizations don't need a full time CFO until revenue is between $25 million to $75 million depending on the complexity of the business and the talent level of the Controller. The numbers just aren't big enough on the financial statements to warrant that kind of salary expense. However, nearly all businesses can benefit from the guidance from a part-time CFO, and there are plenty of them in the market.

There are some minimum-scope tasks and responsibilities a CFO should do every month, except for small organizations where these potentially could be done quarterly. I call this the "regular rhythm" for a part-time CFO.

- Look through the financial statements, or in some situations even the transaction list each month. Develop an understanding of "the story" the numbers are telling about the business recently.

- Talk with the bookkeeper or head of accounting. Discuss the financial results. Ask if there are any areas of specific challenge that the bookkeeper has encountered since the last conversation with the CFO.

- Talk with the CEO or management team about the financial results and the latest health of the business. Deliver the

CFO perspective and the cliff notes version of the financial situation. Acquire information about the operations of the business that could be impacting the numbers.

These tasks are typically smooth and steady, within a fixed and predictable range of time required for each period.

There are many tasks and responsibilities that a CFO could perform outside of the regular rhythm.

- Design and develop a financial statement or management reporting package to be prepared monthly.

- Coach the bookkeeper or head of accounting on best practices in accounting processes and month end close.

- Develop a forecast, and ideally a monthly recurring forecast- update routine.

- Teach others in the organization about the finances of the business, how to understand financial statements, and how to make decisions that improve the financial health of the organization.

- Identify key performance indicators. Design a process for them to be reported and analyzed regularly.

- Manage cash so the current and future balances of cash are understood. If appropriate, implement a short-term weekly cash flow or 13-week cash flow forecast process.

- Manage banking relationships. Lead the process of acquiring or renewing the company's line of credit. These tasks are more discretionary than the regular rhythm, and should be performed when the value to the company exceeds the cost.

Implementing all of these things can pack a lot of effort into a short period if completed in a hurry at the beginning of a new relationship. It is recommended that most businesses identify and list the needs, prioritize them, consider the impact of each on the available time of the CFO, and discuss a plan for when each would be accomplished. Many part-time CFOs are paid by the hour, so spreading these initiatives over many months can keep near-term cost lower compared to doing too much at once. I typically recommend a "smooth and steady" approach of constant improvement, but at a reasonable and affordable pace.

At a small, simple business the need for a part-time CFO might only be a few hours a month to look over the financial results, provide some mentorship to the bookkeeper or head of accounting, and confer with the CEO about the financial health of the business. Check out our company's Virtual CFO program which works with businesses around the country to provide this light scope of financial oversight each month.

For companies that aren't ready for a Virtual CFO, we offer a membership program that builds a relationship between the CEO and one of our experts. This includes a monthly discussion about the business, finances, and accounting processes. We have found that companies with some kind of CFO guidance are significantly more successful than those without it, so our variety of programs are designed to offer support for every size of business at every budget.

Regardless of who you work with, though, the goal should be to maximize success and the business's ability to fulfill the goals of the business owner. Our team is here to help, but most important is for you, the business owner, to find someone you trust who has the expertise, experience, and ability to provide the finance-oriented support you and your company need.

Start by asking people you trust in business for referrals. Then, just as you would for any person you're considering adding to your team, prepare questions well in advance to challenge that individual during the interview process so you can get a clear sense of his or her sweet spot compared to any gaps in expertise.

Our website, www.TheNumbersEdge.com, has some questions and information available for interviewing and hiring accountants.

The ultimate success of your business depends on many things. Mostly, it depends on you. Take responsibility to improve your understanding of the critical areas of the business where your experience is minimal, and learn from the mistakes and experiences of others before you make those mistakes yourself and learn the hard way.

On your path to becoming an experienced, successful business owner, when you don't get the results you want from a decision or situation, you will gain knowhow one way or another because failures grow knowledge much faster than success.

Good luck with your quest and your journey . . . and let me know how I can help you along the way.